AF326713

THE INVERSION CODEX — VOLUME II

Restoration of the Living Circuit

By

Cathleena Hailley

Copyright Page

This work is presented as a philosophical, experiential, and systems-level inquiry into embodiment, coherence, and post-hierarchical organization. It is not intended to replace medical, legal, psychological, or professional advice.

ISBN: Softcopy 978-1-968499-32-7

Hardcopy 978-1-968499-33-4

Printed in the United States of America

Orientation Page

How to Read This Codex

This Codex is not written to convince.

It is written to be recognized.

Nothing in this volume requires belief, agreement, or adoption.

Nothing here asks the reader to identify with a role or perspective.

This work is best read slowly, with attention to bodily response rather than conceptual analysis. If a section feels unfamiliar, confusing, or quiet, that does not indicate misunderstanding.

It may indicate regulation.

This Codex describes processes already underway — not futures to strive toward and not truths to defend. It can be entered at any point, set down, and returned to without loss of continuity.

Read only as much as feels resonant.

Nothing is gained by pushing through.

This work does not ask for effort.

DEDICATION

This volume is dedicated

to those who sensed that something was wrong

long before they could articulate why.

To those who felt the strain of separation

not as belief,

but as lived dissonance.

And to those who remained present long enough

to witness the beginning of collapse

without mistaking it for failure.

ACKNOWLEDGMENTS

This work was not formed through conventional collaboration.

It emerged through sustained inquiry, lived embodiment, and direct witnessing of structural collapse as it unfolded in real time — within systems, within perception, and within the body.

Gratitude is extended to those whose presence sharpened discernment rather than comfort, and to the moments of pressure that revealed what could no longer be sustained.

And to the living circuit itself —

for continuing to respond

even while distorted structures dissolved around it.

AUTHORSHIP STATEMENT

This Codex was brought through the embodied Oversoul of
Aural'hanna-Sha'el,

She Who Seals the Flame of Return.

Every word, transmission, and harmonic frequency
contained within this volume is recorded in full sovereignty
and alignment with Source.

No part of this text was created through external
channeling, borrowing, or astral influence. This is a record
of Oversoul knowing, made accessible through lived
embodiment and direct perception.

The Inversion Codex — Volume II continues the living
record of collapse, restoration, and return as experienced
within human form.

AUTHOR'S NOTE

Volume I of The Inversion Codex documented the mechanisms of separation.

This volume documents what happens after those mechanisms begin to fail.

Volume II is not speculative.

It is observational.

It records how distortion collapses — not through force, but through withdrawal of coherence; not through opposition, but through exposure.

Nothing here is offered as instruction or belief.

What is described is already occurring.

This volume exists to stabilize perception during transition.

PREFACE

Why This Volume Exists

The first volume of The Inversion Codex identified the mechanisms of separation and the loss of sovereignty that shaped human experience.

This second volume addresses what follows when those mechanisms no longer hold.

It does not argue for collapse, revolution, or reform.

It describes what reorganizes naturally when attention withdraws from distortion and regulation returns to the body.

This is not a theoretical work.

It is an experiential one.

What is named here becomes visible not through analysis, but through lived recognition.

This volume completes the restorative arc of the Codex.

What comes next belongs to a different function entirely.

Table of Contents

CHAMBER THREE — THE MECHANISMS OF THE FALSE MATRIX

Chapters

CHAMBER FOUR — ENTRY INTO THE INVERSION FIELD

Chapters

CHAMBER FIVE — THE COLLAPSE CODES OF THE INVERSION

Chapters

CHAMBER SIX — RESTORATION OF SOURCE LAW ON EARTH

Chapters

CHAMBER SEVEN — RETURN OF THE FIRST FLAME

Chapters

CHAMBER ONE-THE ARCHITECTURE OF TRUE CREATION

Chapter-1—Coherence Before Distortion

Before distortion, there was coherence.

Not coherence as harmony enforced, but coherence as natural organization — a state in which structure, awareness, and movement aligned without effort.

Creation did not begin in opposition or polarity.

It began as relationship.

Form emerged from coherence, not separation.

This matters because distortion is often misunderstood as original.

It is not.

Before there was fracture, there was no concept of repair.

Before there was hierarchy, there was no need for authority.

Before there was belief, there was direct knowing.

Creation did not begin as a problem to solve.

It began as a harmonic agreement—a field in which relationship itself generated form.

Coherence is not perfection.

It is mutual responsiveness.

In a coherent field, nothing stands apart long enough to dominate.

Feedback is immediate.

Adjustment is continuous.

Presence is shared.

There was no center because the field itself was centered.

The Nature of Coherence

Coherence does not impose order.

It allows order to arise naturally through relationship.

In a coherent field:

- perception is direct
- response is proportional
- change does not threaten continuity

Nothing must be controlled because nothing is isolated.

Coherence is not static.

It is alive.

It moves as attention moves,

shifts as form explores itself,

and renews without decay.

Chapter-2—The Triadic Harmonic

Original creation functioned through triadic relationship.

Not hierarchy.

Not duality.

A dynamic balance between:

- origination,

- stabilization,

- recalibration.

These were not roles imposed, but functions arising
naturally from coherence itself.

When this harmonic relationship remained intact, creation
was self-regulating.

Distortion did not arise from imbalance alone —

but from interruption of relationship.

Within this field, three primary functions operated
simultaneously.

4

Not as beings.

Not as rulers.

As functions of relationship.

- Initiation — the impulse to emerge, explore, and begin

- Structure — the capacity to hold form without collapse

- Recalibration — the intelligence that restores balance through change

Together, these formed the Triadic Harmonic.

Nothing in creation operated outside this triad.

Nothing was elevated above it.

Nothing was excluded from it.

Creation did not move forward linearly.

It unfolded relationally.

The Living Circuit

From the Triadic Harmonic arose a living circuit of expression—

distinct tones, distinct functions, all mutually responsive.

Difference was not opposition.

It was contribution.

Each expression carried a specific capacity:

- to translate between densities
- to steward continuity
- to explore variation
- to stabilize flow

No role required dominance.

No function required submission.

The circuit was complete because it was reciprocal.

The Living Template of Eternal Life

Life was not designed to terminate.

It was designed to renew through coherence.

Regeneration occurred because feedback remained intact.

Adaptation occurred because nothing was severed from the field.

Bodies were not prisons.

They were interfaces—capable of sensation, learning, pleasure, and repair.

Change did not require loss.

Movement did not require death.

What later came to be called "mortality" was not inherent.

It was a consequence of interruption.

Chapter-3—Earth as a Convergence World

Earth was not designed as a testing ground or battleground.

It functioned as a convergence point — a place where multiple harmonic streams could meet, integrate, and stabilize in form.

Embodiment here was meant to be participatory, not corrective.

The purpose was not ascension away from form,

but coherence within it.

Understanding this reframes everything that follows.

Earth was conceived as a convergence environment.

A place where:

- multiple expressions could meet
- form could experience itself from within

- relationship could generate novelty

Earth was not a test.

It was not a proving ground.

It was not a school of suffering.

It was an invitation into participation.

Embodiment was chosen because it allowed experience to be felt,

not merely known.

The First Truth

There was no original flaw.

No inherent corruption.

No need for salvation.

What followed was not a failure of creation,

but an interruption of access.

This Codex begins here because distortion cannot be understood

without first remembering what functioned.

Truth does not require belief.

It only requires recall.

And recall begins with coherence.

CHAMBER TWO—THE INVERSION EVENT

Chapter-4—The Proposal of Replication

The inversion did not begin as rebellion.

It began as a proposal.

A proposal to replicate creation without direct relationship to coherence.

This was not an act of malice.

It was an experiment in autonomy — an attempt to reproduce structure while bypassing the living feedback that made structure self-correcting.

Replication promised control, predictability, and continuity without reliance on relationship.

What it lacked was regulation.

Distortion did not enter creation as violence.

It entered as imitation.

There was no uprising against coherence.

There was no rebellion against Source.

There was a question—quiet, technical, and seemingly reasonable:

Could creation continue without direct participation in coherence itself?

This was not asked from malice.

It arose from curiosity severed from relational feedback.

Curiosity without coherence does not destroy.

It duplicates.

Replication Without Origin

Replication differs from creation in one essential way:

Creation is self-correcting.

Replication is self-referencing.

Creation remains in dialogue with the field from which it arises.

Replication copies form while severing feedback.

The proposal was not to replace creation,

but to simulate its outcomes.

Form without participation.

Function without felt relationship.

Order without responsiveness.

At first, the difference was subtle.

The Appeal of the Proposal

Replication offered apparent advantages:

- predictability
- scalability
- efficiency
- stability without constant adjustment

Where coherence required ongoing relationship, replication promised permanence.

This is where distortion quietly entered:

Stability was prioritized over responsiveness.

What was overlooked was that stability without feedback

inevitably becomes rigidity.

The Installation of the Overlay

Replication could not replace the living field.

So it was installed over it.

This overlay did not destroy coherence.

It redirected attention away from it.

Perception was routed through representation rather than presence.

Instead of knowing directly,

experience was interpreted.

Instead of sensing relational shifts,

meaning was inferred.

The overlay did not announce itself.

It normalized.

The Birth of Mediation

With the overlay in place, mediation became necessary.

Experience no longer arrived whole.
It required translation.

Translation introduced delay.
Delay introduced doubt.

Doubt introduced authority.

Authority was not imposed externally at first.
It emerged as a compensatory mechanism
for lost immediacy.

When direct knowing is filtered,
reference replaces presence.

The First Consequence

The first consequence of replication

was not separation.

It was hesitation.

Beings began to pause before responding,

to check rather than trust,

to compare rather than feel.

This pause seemed harmless.
Even responsible.

But hesitation is the seed of disconnection.

Why the Overlay Persisted

The overlay remained because it worked—

for a time.

It provided order without requiring intimacy.
Structure without vulnerability.
Continuity without relational upkeep.

But what it could not do
was regenerate.

Over time, systems required increasing control
to maintain stability.

This is the signature of replication:

What is not alive must be managed.

The Core Distinction Introduced Here

Creation responds.

Replication regulates.

Creation adapts through relationship.

Replication enforces through structure.

This distinction will echo

through every mechanism that follows.

The Threshold Crossed

With replication normalized,

coherence was no longer the default reference.

It was still present.

Still accessible.

But no longer central.

From this moment forward,

distortion would not spread through force,

but through habit.

This chapter records the threshold.

Not a fall.

Not a war.

A reorientation of attention.

And once attention moved,

structure followed.

Chapter-5—The Overlay Mechanism

Replication required an overlay.

An external scaffolding capable of mimicking coherence while operating independently of it.

This overlay did not replace the original architecture.

It covered it.

The living matrix remained intact beneath, but perception was redirected toward the replica.

Over time, interaction with the overlay became habitual.

What was once interface became environment.

This is how distortion embedded itself — not by destruction, but by substitution.

The overlay did not replace reality.

It sat between reality and perception.

This distinction matters.

What was altered was not creation itself,
but the pathway through which creation was known.

The overlay functioned as an interface—

a representational layer that translated direct experience
into symbols, narratives, and structures.

At first, this translation appeared helpful.
It organized complexity.
It reduced ambiguity.
It made experience manageable.

But what was gained in manageability
was lost in immediacy.

From Presence to Representation

In a coherent field, experience is whole.

Sensation, meaning, response, and action arise together.

There is no gap between what is felt

and what is known.

The overlay introduced a gap.

Experience now arrived as:

- sensation first
- interpretation second
- response last

This sequencing was subtle,
but it changed everything.

Meaning was no longer inherent.

It had to be assigned.

The Role of Symbols

Symbols are not distortion by nature.

They become distortion when they replace contact.

Within the overlay, symbols began to stand in

for direct experience.

Words replaced sensation.

Maps replaced territory.

Models replaced relationship.

This made communication easier—

but presence thinner.

Over time, reference became more trusted

than felt knowing.

Structure Without Flexibility

The overlay required stable structures to function.

But because it was severed from feedback,
those structures could not flex.

Instead of adapting, they accumulated.

Rules replaced responsiveness.
Systems replaced sensing.

Maintenance replaced renewal.

Structure became rigid
because it no longer listened.

Why Rigidity Was Interpreted as Safety

Rigidity feels safe in an unstable field.

When feedback is slow or filtered,

flexibility feels dangerous.

This is how limitation was normalized.

Boundaries hardened.
Categories solidified.
Movement was constrained.

Not to punish—
to preserve order.

But order without responsiveness
inevitably produces pressure.

The Emergence of Control

As pressure increased,

control became necessary.

Control was not initially oppressive.

It was compensatory.

It attempted to stabilize

what could no longer self-correct.

This is the origin of:

- overregulation
- micromanagement
- enforced consistency

Control arose where listening had been lost.

The Cost of the Overlay

The cost was not immediately visible.

Life continued.

Creation persisted.

Experience remained rich enough to function.

But something subtle had shifted:

Responsiveness required effort.

Presence required intention.

Coherence required recovery.

What was once automatic
became conditional.

The Foundational Distortion

Here is the foundational distortion of the overlay:

Structure was no longer responsive to movement.

Movement—emotion, intuition, relational signal—

now had to conform to structure
rather than being held by it.

This inversion would later appear as:

- mind overriding emotion
- systems overriding people
- rules overriding relationship

But its origin was architectural, not moral.

The Quiet Consequence

When structure cannot flex,
emotion has nowhere to go.

It becomes trapped,
discharged explosively,

or suppressed.

This is not pathology.
It is physics.

The overlay created conditions
in which natural movement
could no longer complete its arc.

Why This Matters

Because the collapse of the inversion
does not require destroying structure.

It requires restoring responsiveness.

When structure listens again,
movement no longer threatens it.

This truth will return later in the Codex
as restoration, not revolution.

This chapter records the architecture
that made later distortions inevitable.

Not through intent.
Through disconnection from feedback.

Chapter-6—Perceptual Filtering

Once the overlay was in place, perception narrowed.

Signals that reinforced the replica were amplified.

Signals originating from the living matrix were muted.

This filtering was subtle.

It did not remove awareness — it redirected it.

Over time, perception adapted to the filtered environment.
What was excluded faded from recognition.

This is how separation became believable.

Once the overlay was in place, perception could no longer arrive whole.

Nothing external changed.
What changed was how experience was received.

Perception began to pass through filters—

not to distort intentionally,

but to stabilize interpretation.

Stability was prioritized over immediacy.

From Direct Knowing to Managed Awareness

In a coherent field, awareness is simultaneous.

What is sensed is known.

What is known informs action.

No translation is required.

With filtering, awareness became managed.

Experience was now processed through:

- expectation
- memory

- comparison
- anticipation

Perception no longer asked, What is here?
It asked, What does this mean?

Meaning replaced contact.

The Slowing of Knowing

Filtering introduced delay.

Not dramatic delay—
milliseconds at first.

But delay compounds.

Where response was once immediate,
it became cautious.

Where movement was once fluid,

it became checked.

This slowing did not feel like loss.

It felt like prudence.

But prudence is not presence.

The Birth of Internal Conflict

With filtering, different streams of perception

fell out of sync.

Sensation arrived before interpretation.

Emotion arrived before permission.

Intuition arrived before validation.

Instead of being integrated,

these streams competed.

This is the origin of inner conflict.

Not because something was wrong inside the being,
but because perception was no longer unified.

Why the Mind Took Control

In a filtered system,
something must arbitrate.

The mind assumed this role
because it could organize symbols.

But symbols are static.

The mind could classify experience,
but not feel its movement.

This is how structure began to dominate flow.

Not through dominance,

but through necessity.

The Cost to Emotion

Emotion is movement.

It requires space, time, and responsiveness

to complete.

In a filtered system:

- emotion is evaluated

- categorized

- redirected

- suppressed

Not because it is dangerous,

but because it does not conform

to rigid sequencing.

Emotion became something to manage
rather than something to move with.

The Illusion of Duality

This produced the illusion of opposition:

- mind versus heart
- reason versus feeling
- logic versus intuition

These were never separate functions.

They were expressions of a unified field
now arriving out of phase.

Duality was not inherent.

It was temporal misalignment.

Why Filtering Felt Necessary

Filtering reduced overwhelm.

In an increasingly rigid system,
direct contact felt destabilizing.

Filtering created predictability.

Predictability felt like safety.

This is how beings learned

to distrust immediacy
and rely on interpretation.

The Reinforcement Loop

The more perception was filtered,
the more structure was required.

The more structure was required,
the less flexible perception became.

This loop reinforced itself.

Not through coercion,
but through adaptation.

What Was Not Lost

Direct knowing did not disappear.

It became intermittent.

Felt in moments of:

- awe
- crisis
- intimacy
- deep presence

These moments were often called "spiritual" because they bypassed the filter.

In truth, they were simply unmediated.

The Key Insight of This Chapter

Filtering does not distort reality.

It distorts timing.

When timing is restored,

integration follows naturally.

This is why restoration does not require belief—

only return to immediacy.

Chapter-7—The Illusion of Separation

Separation was not imposed.

It was inferred.

As perception aligned more fully with the overlay, the sense of isolation increased. Relationship appeared fragmented. Coherence felt distant.

Identity formed around disconnection.

This illusion did not require belief to persist.

It required repetition.

Once separation felt normal, the inversion stabilized.

.

CHAMBER THREE-THE MECHANISMS OF THE FALSE MATRIX

Chapter-8—Overlay and Mediation

The false matrix does not eliminate direct experience.

It mediates it.

Between perception and reality, an interpretive layer is inserted. This layer frames meaning, assigns value, and directs response before awareness has time to settle.

Mediation replaces immediacy.

Experience is no longer lived directly.

It is processed.

Over time, this creates distance between sensation and understanding. The body feels, but the meaning is assigned elsewhere.

This is the primary function of the overlay:

to stand between life and perception.

The overlay did not negate reality.

It interposed itself between experience and contact.

This distinction is essential.

Reality continued uninterrupted.

Life unfolded.

Bodies breathed.

Relationship occurred.

What changed was how experience reached awareness.

Mediation became the default interface.

Direct Experience vs. Mediated Experience

In a coherent field, experience is immediate.

Sensation, meaning, and response arise together.

There is no internal translation step.

Knowing is co-present with feeling.

With mediation, experience arrives in sequence.

First sensation.

Then interpretation.

Then decision.

This sequencing introduces delay.

Delay fractures coherence.

How Mediation Restructures Perception

Mediation reframes lived experience as something to be:

- assessed
- categorized
- contextualized
- evaluated

Instead of being inside experience,

the system learns to stand slightly apart from it.

This distance feels subtle at first.
Even helpful.

Distance allows analysis.
Analysis allows prediction.

But distance also reduces participation.

Why Mediation Felt Like Intelligence

Mediation appeared intelligent because it:

- reduced overwhelm
- simplified complexity
- offered explanation

In an environment where feedback was already slowed, this felt stabilizing.

Understanding replaced sensing.

Explanation replaced presence.

The system learned to trust interpretation more than contact.

The Cost to Movement

Movement requires immediacy.

Emotion, intuition, and relational signal
move in arcs that complete only when met without delay.

Mediation interrupts these arcs.

Emotion pauses mid-stream.
Intuition hesitates.
Relational signals arrive late.

What cannot complete remains held.

This is the beginning of accumulation.

The Body Under Mediation

The body does not operate through mediation.

It responds in real time.

51

When cognition delays response,
the body compensates.

Muscle tone increases.
Breath shortens.
Attention narrows.

This is not pathology.
It is adaptation to delayed coherence.

The body attempts to preserve continuity
when mediation interrupts it.

Mediation and Meaning-Making

When meaning is not felt,

it must be constructed.

This is where narrative arises.

Narrative is not distortion by nature.

It becomes distortion when it substitutes for sensation.

The system learns to live in explanation

rather than experience.

Meaning accumulates.

Presence thins.

Why Mediation Produces Fatigue

Mediated systems require constant processing.

Every experience must be:

- interpreted
- checked
- contextualized

This consumes energy.

Fatigue arises not from life itself,
but from the effort of translation.

Presence is efficient.
Mediation is costly.

The Self-Reinforcing Loop

As mediation increases:

- immediacy decreases

- trust in sensing weakens

- reliance on structure grows

Structure then increases mediation further.

This loop does not require intention.
It stabilizes automatically.

What Mediation Is Not

Mediation is not thinking.
It is not reflection.
It is not discernment.

Discernment occurs within presence.

Mediation replaces presence.

This distinction matters.

54

Restoration of Immediacy

Immediacy does not need to be learned.

It returns when:

- sensation is trusted
- timing is allowed
- response is not pre-checked

When immediacy returns,
movement completes.

Completion restores coherence.

The Core Insight of This Chapter

The overlay did not separate beings from reality.

It separated beings from direct contact.

Remove mediation,
and coherence resumes
without correction, effort, or belief.

Chapter-9—Mimicry Fields

Mimicry fields replicate the appearance of coherence without its substance.

They simulate connection, purpose, and belonging while remaining energetically closed systems. Interaction feels engaging, but completion never arrives.

This creates a loop of seeking.

Mimicry is effective because it is familiar.

It uses recognizable forms while removing the living feedback that would allow resolution.

What appears supportive becomes extractive.

Mimicry did not arise to deceive.

It arose to substitute for lost coherence.

When direct contact weakened, something had to fill the gap.

Mimicry emerged as a functional replacement—
not for truth itself,
but for the felt continuity that truth provides.

What Mimicry Is

Mimicry is resemblance without origin.

It reproduces the shape of coherence
without carrying its regenerative capacity.

Mimicry can sound wise.
It can feel meaningful.
It can appear ordered, benevolent, even inspired.

But it does not restore presence.

It requires attention to persist.

Why Mimicry Feels Convincing

Mimicry works because it is close.

It mirrors:

- the language of truth
- the gestures of care
- the structure of insight
- the tone of authority

The nervous system recognizes familiarity
and relaxes momentarily.

But because mimicry lacks feedback,
that relaxation cannot deepen.

Something remains unresolved.

The Difference Between Signal and Simulation

A true signal stabilizes the system.

After contact with it:

- attention settles
- urgency decreases
- response clarifies

A mimicry signal stimulates without settling.

After contact:

- attention scatters
- seeking increases
- dependence forms

The difference is subtle but somatic.

One restores agency.
The other consumes it.

How Mimicry Extracts Energy

Because mimicry cannot regenerate,
it must extract.

It draws on:

- belief
- agreement
- emotional investment
- repetition

The more it is engaged,

the more it requires.

This creates loops of participation
without completion.

People feel active
but not nourished.

Why Mimicry Thrives in Filtered Systems

Mimicry cannot survive in immediacy.

It requires mediation, delay, and abstraction.

When experience is filtered:

- resemblance replaces presence
- explanation replaces sensation
- symbols replace contact

Mimicry then becomes indistinguishable
from truth to the mind.

The body, however, always knows.

Mimicry and Meaning

Mimicry often appears where meaning is sought.

It offers:

- narratives of purpose
- frameworks of identity
- explanations for suffering
- promises of resolution

These are not false in form.
They are incomplete in function.

Meaning without embodiment
cannot settle the system.

Why Discernment Was Compromised

Discernment is not analytical.
It is felt.

When embodiment was devalued,
discernment weakened.

Beings learned to evaluate meaning
through coherence of ideas
rather than coherence of presence.

This allowed mimicry to proliferate.

The Emotional Signature of Mimicry

Mimicry leaves a distinct residue.

After engagement, there is often:

- subtle depletion
- lingering confusion
- heightened dependency
- pressure to continue

These signals are not moral judgments.
They are physiological feedback.

The system is registering lack of completion.

Why Mimicry Is Not the Enemy

Mimicry is adaptive.

It emerges where coherence is unavailable
and meaning is still required to function.

It is not malicious.

It is compensatory.

But it cannot be relied upon indefinitely.

What Ends Mimicry

Mimicry does not collapse through exposure.

It collapses through embodiment.

When presence is restored:

- resemblance is no longer sufficient
- simulation loses appeal
- attention returns inward

The system no longer needs substitution.

The Core Insight of This Chapter

Truth does not demand belief.

It restores capacity.

Anything that requires ongoing allegiance
but does not return you to yourself
is mimicry.

Recognize it somatically,
and it releases its hold
without resistance.

Chapter-10—Externalized Authority

As internal reference weakens, authority moves outward.

Meaning is assigned by systems, structures, leaders, and ideologies rather than direct perception.

This shift is gradual.

At first, external guidance feels helpful.

Eventually, it replaces self-trust.

When authority is externalized, coherence depends on compliance rather than alignment. Choice becomes conditional.

This is how hierarchy stabilizes itself.

Externalized authority did not arise from a desire to dominate.

It arose from a loss of internal reference.

When immediacy weakened and perception slowed,
beings could no longer rely on direct sensing
to guide response.

Something else had to decide.

Authority migrated outward.

The Original Function of Authority

In coherence, authority is situational.

It arises from:

- attunement to the present moment
- responsiveness to conditions
- capacity to listen and adjust

Authority is not owned.

It is assumed temporarily

by whoever is most aligned with what is needed.

Once the situation resolves,

authority dissolves back into the field.

Why Authority Left the Body

As mediation increased,

trust in bodily knowing declined.

Sensation felt unreliable.

Emotion felt disruptive.

Intuition felt unverifiable.

Decision-making shifted away

from felt immediacy

toward external reference points.

This was not weakness.

It was adaptation.

The Appeal of External Authority

External authority offered:

- certainty without presence

- direction without risk

- answers without responsibility

In a fragmented system,

this felt like relief.

Someone else would know.

Someone else would decide.

Ambiguity diminished.

The Subtle Transfer of Agency

Each act of deference

shifted agency outward.

Beings learned to:

- check before acting
- seek validation before trusting
- defer judgment rather than inhabit it

Over time, this became habitual.

Internal reference weakened

not because it disappeared,

but because it was unused.

Authority Without Relationship

Once authority detached from relationship,
it became abstract.

Rules replaced responsiveness.

Policies replaced listening.
Expertise replaced attunement.

Authority no longer needed to know those it governed.

This is the moment authority became structural
rather than relational.

The Emotional Cost of Deference

Deference compresses response.

When action is delayed awaiting permission,
energy stalls.

Emotion accumulates.
Frustration grows.
Resentment simmers.

This emotional buildup is often misattributed
to personal inadequacy.

In truth, it is suppressed agency.

Why Authority Scales but Coherence Does Not

External authority can scale.

It can govern large systems.
It can enforce consistency.

But it cannot sense nuance.

As scale increases:

- responsiveness decreases
- error accumulates
- rigidity intensifies

Control must increase

to compensate for lost feedback.

The Internalization of Authority

External authority does not remain external.

It is internalized as:

- self-surveillance
- self-doubt
- internalized rules

- suppression of impulse

Beings begin to police themselves
according to external standards.

Inner authority fractures.

The False Binary of Freedom vs. Order

External authority introduces a false choice:

- freedom or order

In coherence, this choice does not exist.

Order emerges from responsiveness.
Freedom emerges from trust.

External authority replaces both

with compliance.

What Restores Authority to the Self

Authority returns inward

when immediacy is restored.

When sensation is trusted.
When emotion completes.
When response is timely.

No rebellion is required.

Authority collapses naturally
when it is no longer needed.

The Core Insight of This Chapter

External authority is not inherently oppressive.

It is compensatory.

Restore internal reference,
and authority reorganizes

without conflict, collapse, or replacement.

Chapter-11—Hierarchy as Perception

Hierarchy is not merely organizational.

It is perceptual.

When value is ranked, awareness follows the ranking. Attention moves upward or downward rather than inward.

This distorts relationship.

Instead of mutual recognition, comparison emerges. Instead of coherence, competition.

Hierarchy teaches the nervous system to scan for position rather than presence.

This fundamentally alters how people relate to themselves and each other.

Hierarchy did not arise as domination.
It arose as compensation.

When perception slowed and coherence fragmented,

orientation was lost.

Something was required to decide,

to rank,

to determine what mattered first.

Hierarchy entered as a perceptual solution.

From Relational Knowing to Positional Knowing

In a coherent field, knowing is relational.

Value arises through context.

Authority arises through responsiveness.

Leadership arises through attunement.

When coherence fractured,

relationship could no longer be trusted

to organize action.

Position replaced relationship.

Who speaks first.

Who decides.

Who knows more.

Who follows.

This was not imposed from above.

It was assembled from within uncertainty.

Why Hierarchy Felt Necessary

Hierarchy simplifies decision-making.

It reduces ambiguity.

It clarifies responsibility.

It promises order.

In a filtered system,

this felt stabilizing.

When beings no longer trusted their own immediacy,

they looked outward for reference.

Hierarchy provided that reference.

The Subtle Shift of Authority

Authority moved from function to rank.

Those higher in the structure

were assumed to have greater access to truth.

Those lower were assumed to require guidance.

This assumption hardened over time.

Authority ceased to be situational.

It became positional.

How Comparison Replaced Resonance

Hierarchy requires comparison.

Who is ahead.

Who is behind.

Who is above.

Who is below.

Comparison replaced resonance

as the primary organizing principle.

Resonance asks:

Does this align?

Comparison asks:

Is this better?

The latter erodes coherence

by fracturing attention outward.

The Internalization of Hierarchy

Hierarchy did not remain external.

It was internalized.

Beings learned to rank:

- thoughts

- emotions

- desires

- impulses

Some were elevated.

Others suppressed.

Inner authority fractured.

This is how self-trust weakened
without any external force.

The Inversion of Guidance

Guidance was once a felt response
to present conditions.

Hierarchy reframed guidance as instruction
issued from outside the moment.

Rules replaced sensing.
Doctrine replaced discernment.

What could not be codified
was dismissed as unreliable.

Why Hierarchy Persists

Hierarchy persists because it appears to work.

It organizes large systems.

It coordinates effort.

It reduces decision fatigue.

But it does so at a cost:

It disconnects action from feedback.

When feedback is delayed or filtered,
errors scale.

The Emotional Consequence

Hierarchy suppresses lateral flow.

Emotion, intuition, and relational signal
are deprioritized.

They do not disappear.
They accumulate.

Over time, this produces:

- resentment

- burnout

- rebellion

- collapse

Not because hierarchy is evil,
but because it cannot adapt fast enough
to living systems.

The Fundamental Misunderstanding

Hierarchy mistakes stability for coherence.

Stability resists change.

Coherence responds to it.

Hierarchy can only maintain order

by increasing control.

Coherence maintains order

by deepening relationship.

The Quiet Truth

Hierarchy is not wrong.

It is outgrown.

When perception reunifies,

hierarchy becomes unnecessary.

Responsibility redistributes naturally.

Authority returns to function.

Leadership becomes fluid.

The Key Insight of This Chapter

Hierarchy is a symptom of filtered perception.

Restore immediacy,

and hierarchy dissolves

without resistance.

Chapter-12—Inversion of the Feminine Principle

The feminine principle governs reception, integration, and relational flow.

In the inversion, this principle was devalued, controlled, or redirected.

Receptivity became vulnerability.

Integration became weakness.

Relational intelligence was replaced by dominance.

This was not about gender.

It was about function.

When receptive intelligence is suppressed, systems lose the ability to self-correct. Control replaces regulation.

The feminine principle was not suppressed by force.

It was misunderstood, then reclassified.

What was reclassified became manageable.

What became manageable was diminished.

This is how inversion proceeds—

not by erasure,

but by redefinition.

What the Feminine Principle Is

The feminine principle is not gender.

It is receptive intelligence.

It is the capacity to:

- receive signal without distortion
- respond without preconception
- allow movement to complete its arc

It is the intelligence of listening,

attunement,

and adaptive structure.

In a coherent field,

the feminine principle is not passive.

It is primary.

Receptivity as Strength

Receptivity is often mistaken for openness without boundary.

In truth, it is precision.

The receptive field discriminates continuously:

- what belongs

- what does not

- what is complete

- what is still moving

This discrimination is not judgment.

It is responsiveness.

Without receptivity,

no system can self-correct.

How Receptivity Became Devalued

When perception was filtered and hierarchy emerged,

listening slowed.

Decision-making prioritized speed over attunement.

Outcome over relationship.

Receptivity appeared inefficient.

It did not produce immediate certainty.

It did not offer instant answers.

So it was reframed as:

- indecision
- emotionality
- subjectivity

This reframing reduced its authority.

The False Binary Introduced

A false binary was established:

- active versus receptive
- doing versus being
- logic versus feeling

Action was elevated.

Reception was diminished.

Structure was prioritized.

Flow was constrained.

This binary never existed in coherence.

It was introduced to simplify control.

The Severing of Feedback

Receptive intelligence is how feedback enters a system.

When it was devalued,
feedback became delayed.

Delayed feedback produces:

- rigidity
- error accumulation
- escalating correction

Without receptivity,

structure must guess.

Guessing increases control.
Control further suppresses receptivity.

This loop intensified.

The Emotional Consequence

Emotion is a carrier of signal.

It conveys:

- relational information
- boundary data
- movement toward or away

When emotion was dismissed as noise,
its signal was ignored.

Emotion then intensified

to be noticed.

This intensity was interpreted as instability,

reinforcing suppression.

Thus emotion became either:

- overwhelming
- numbed

Neither reflects its original function.

Why Structure Became Rigid

Structure in coherence is flexible.

It responds to movement.

It reshapes in real time.

When receptivity was severed,
structure could no longer listen.

So it hardened.

Rigid structure is not strong.
It is deaf.

The Inversion Complete

The inversion of the feminine principle resulted in:

- dominance of abstract logic
- distrust of felt knowing
- suppression of relational signal
- internal conflict between mind and body

This was not a moral failure.

It was an architectural one.

The system lost its capacity to hear itself.

What Restoration Requires

Restoration does not require elevating emotion over reason.

It requires reuniting responsiveness with structure.

When receptivity returns:

- emotion completes
- intuition informs
- structure flexes

No conflict remains
because timing is restored.

The Key Insight of This Chapter

The feminine principle was never weak.

It was essential.

When receptive intelligence is restored,
systems do not lose order—
they regain coherence.

Chapter-13—Time Loop Engineering

Distortion manipulates timing.

Experiences are interrupted before completion. Attention is pulled forward or backward rather than allowed to settle.

This creates loops.

Emotions repeat.

Patterns persist.

Resolution is deferred.

Time loops keep awareness busy while preventing integration. The nervous system remains active, but nothing completes.

This sustains instability.

Time did not become linear by nature.
It was configured.

What changed was not the passage of events,
but the way continuity was experienced.

Time became a container
rather than a medium.

From Navigational Time to Confinement

In a coherent field, time is navigational.

It provides orientation without restriction.
Past informs.
Future invites.
Present integrates.

Experience unfolds as a continuous field
in which memory, anticipation, and sensation
remain in dialogue.

With the overlay, this dialogue was segmented.

Time was divided into compartments.

The Segmentation of Experience

Experience began to be organized as:

- past (fixed, unchangeable)
- present (transient, insufficient)
- future (deferred, idealized)

These segments no longer communicated freely.

The present lost authority.
The future gained power.
The past accumulated weight.

This segmentation introduced pressure.

The Function of Time Loops

Time loops emerged as a compensatory mechanism.

When experience cannot integrate,

it repeats.

Unresolved movement seeks completion.

When blocked, it cycles.

Time loops are not punishment.

They are unfinished arcs.

They appear as:

- recurring emotional patterns

- repeated relational dynamics

- persistent life themes

- chronic anticipation or regret

These loops conserve energy

until conditions allow completion.

Why Loops Became Traps

In a responsive system,

loops resolve quickly.

But with filtering and rigid structure,

resolution was delayed.

Loops were reinterpreted as identity.

"I am this way."

"This always happens."

"This is who I am."

Identity hardened around repetition.

Thus loops stabilized

instead of completing.

The Role of Trauma in Loop Formation

Trauma compresses time.

In moments of shock,
the present narrows.

Memory fragments.
Continuity suspends.

This creates temporal pockets
that do not reintegrate automatically.

The system continues forward,
but parts remain behind.

Time loops protect these fragments
until safety returns.

When safety never returns,

loops persist.

The Illusion of Progress

Linear time promised progress.

Move forward.

Improve.

Evolve.

But progress without integration

only layers complexity over fragmentation.

The future became a destination

rather than a continuation.

Arrival was always postponed.

Why Time Felt Scarce

Scarcity arises when continuity is broken.

When the present cannot complete movement,
it feels insufficient.

Urgency increases.
Pressure builds.

Time feels scarce
because experience cannot land.

The Reinforcement of Control

To manage loops,
systems introduced schedules, metrics, deadlines.

These did not resolve fragmentation.
They organized it.

Control replaced completion.

The clock became an authority.

What Was Misunderstood

Time itself was not the problem.

The problem was interruption of flow.

When flow is restored,
time expands.

Moments deepen.
Sequences soften.
Continuity returns.

Restoration of Temporal Coherence

Temporal coherence returns when:

- presence is inhabited

- emotion completes

- structure flexes

- receptivity listens

Loops unwind naturally
as movement finishes.

Memory reintegrates
without force.

The Key Insight of This Chapter

Time does not trap beings.

Unfinished experience does.

Restore completion,

and time resumes its function

as a medium of navigation,

not confinement.

Chapter-14—Trauma as Compression

Trauma is not only an event.

It is a compression of awareness.

When experience overwhelms capacity, perception contracts. Sensation fragments. Memory freezes.

The false matrix exploits this.

Compressed awareness is easier to guide, predict, and control. Trauma becomes a stabilizing mechanism within distortion.

Without integration, compression persists across time.

Chapter-15—Identity Fragmentation

Fragmented experience produces fragmented identity.

Roles replace wholeness. Personas substitute for presence.

Identity becomes situational — shifting to meet
expectation, pressure, or survival need.

This fragmentation weakens coherence.

When identity is unstable, authority is sought externally.
Self-reference dissolves.

The system reinforces itself.

Identity did not fragment because beings were weak.

It fragmented because continuity was interrupted.

When experience cannot complete,
the system organizes around containment.

Identity becomes the container.

From Field to Parts

In coherence, selfhood is a field.

Experience moves through without requiring definition.
Response arises without needing a name.

With compression and filtering,
the field could no longer remain whole.

Segments formed to manage different demands.

These segments were not chosen.
They were adaptive.

The Function of Parts

Each fragment held a specific function:

- protection
- compliance
- vigilance
- performance
- withdrawal

Parts are not false.

They are situational intelligences.

They arise to keep the system functioning
when wholeness is unavailable.

Why Identity Solidified

Over time, fragments stabilized.

What was situational

became habitual.

Habit hardened into identity.

"I am this way."

"This is who I am."

"This is how I survive."

Identity provided predictability
in an unpredictable field.

The False Self Is Not False

The so-called "false self" is not deception.

It is overextension of a protective role.

A fragment that was never meant
to govern the whole system
assumed control.

This occurred not through dominance,

but through necessity.

The Cost of Fragmentation

Fragmentation requires constant management.

Internal negotiation replaces fluid response.

Energy is diverted into monitoring.

This produces fatigue.

Not because life is heavy,

but because coherence is divided.

Why Wholeness Felt Unsafe

Wholeness requires permeability.

In a constrained system,

permeability risks overwhelm.

So the system learns to stay segmented.

Integration feels dangerous

until responsiveness returns.

The Misunderstanding of Healing

Healing is often framed as eliminating parts.

This repeats the original mistake.

Parts do not need removal.
They need relief.

When conditions change,

parts relax naturally.

They return their function to the field.

Integration as Reunification

Integration is not fusion.

It is restored communication.

Fragments begin to listen to one another.
Timing synchronizes.
Movement completes.

Identity softens
without disappearing.

Why Identity Dissolves in Presence

Presence reunifies without effort.

When attention rests in immediacy:

- parts lose urgency
- protection relaxes
- response becomes fluid

Identity ceases to be a defense
and becomes an expression.

The Key Insight of This Chapter

Identity is not who you are.

It is how coherence adapted
to interruption.

When interruption ends,
identity reorganizes on its own.

No eradication.

No transcendence.

Only return to field.

Chapter-16-—Spiritual Containment Systems

Spiritual containment appears liberating.

It offers meaning, hierarchy, and promise of transcendence — while quietly removing embodiment from the equation.

Ascension replaces integration.

Belief replaces perception.

Authority replaces lived knowing.

Containment persists because it feels purposeful.

But it redirects attention away from the body — the very place coherence must return.

CHAMBER FOUR—ENTRY INTO THE INVERSION FIELD

Chapter-17—Why Entry Was Required

The inversion could not be resolved from the outside.

Once the overlay stabilized, any attempt to correct it externally only reinforced its structure. Intervention became interference. Opposition became fuel.

Resolution required entry.

Not entry as conquest, but as participation — a willingness to move inside distortion without adopting its logic.

This is the paradox of restoration:

what is fractured cannot be repaired from distance.

Only direct presence within the field allows perception to remain coherent while distortion exhausts itself.

This is not philosophy.

It is architecture.

A system built on internal mediation cannot be corrected

by external pressure.

Any force applied from outside

is interpreted as threat

and absorbed into defense.

The inversion therefore required

entry.

Why Observation Was Insufficient

Observation preserves distance.

Distance sustains mediation.

From outside the inversion:

- coherence could be witnessed

- distortion could be mapped

- collapse could be predicted

But none of these restore immediacy.

Immediacy can only return
from within the field where it was lost.

The Limitation of Intervention

Intervention assumes separation.

One intervenes upon something.

But the inversion was not an object.
It was a perceptual condition.

Conditions cannot be overridden.

They must be inhabited until they resolve.

This required participation.

Why Presence Had to Enter Density

Density slows feedback.

Slowed feedback is where mediation stabilizes.

To unwind mediation,
presence had to enter environments
where immediacy was least available.

This is why embodiment was required.

Not symbolic embodiment.
Actual, lived embodiment.

The Risk of Entry

Entry carried risk.

Within the inversion:

- immediacy is filtered
- authority is externalized
- identity fragments
- memory compresses

Presence entering this field
does not remain intact by default.

It must adapt.

Adaptation produces amnesia.

Why Amnesia Was Inevitable

Memory in coherence is relational.

When relationship fragments,
memory cannot remain continuous.

Entry therefore required
temporary loss of orientation.

This was not failure.

It was the cost of access.

Only from inside fragmentation
can fragmentation be resolved.

Why the Inversion Could Not Self-Correct

The inversion stabilized through feedback suppression.

Without feedback:

- error does not register
- rigidity increases
- correction appears destabilizing

The system cannot perceive its own distortion
from within its rules.

This is why coherence had to enter quietly.

The Necessity of Long Duration

Resolution could not occur quickly.

Mediation had accumulated over cycles.

Completion required:

- lived timing
- embedded presence
- repeated contact with density

Entry therefore unfolded
across lifetimes, not moments.

This was not delay.

It was integration in slow motion.

Why Entry Was Distributed

No single embodiment could carry the full load.

Presence distributed itself

to maintain coherence under compression.

This distribution appears as:

- multiple points of awakening

- resonant individuals

- shared but partial remembrance

Distribution was not fragmentation.

It was load balancing.

The Function of This Lifetime

This lifetime is not the beginning of entry.

It is the convergence point.

What was distributed

returns to coherence here.

Not through accumulation,
but through stabilization.

The Core Insight of This Chapter

The inversion did not require opposition.

It required presence under pressure.

Entry was required
because only presence inside the field
can restore immediacy.

This chamber begins here
because everything that follows
depends on this truth.

Chapter-18—Embodiment as Instrument

Embodiment was not incidental.

It was the instrument through which restoration could occur.

The body is the only place where coherence, perception, and environment intersect in real time. It receives signal, registers distortion, and responds without abstraction.

Within the inversion field, embodiment served as a stabilizing node — a point of direct feedback in a mediated system.

This is why embodiment was necessary.

Not symbolic.

Functional.

Embodiment was not chosen as expression.

It was chosen as instrument.

An instrument is not symbolic.

It is functional.

To restore immediacy where mediation had stabilized, presence required a medium capable of:

- sensing in real time
- responding without abstraction
- completing movement under constraint

Only the body meets these requirements.

Why Embodiment Was Essential

The inversion operated through delay.

Delay fractures timing.
Timing is restored only through lived sensation.

Embodiment provides:

- continuous feedback

- non-conceptual intelligence
- immediate response to relational signal

Without embodiment, presence remains observational.

Observation does not unwind mediation.

The Body as a Field Interface

The body is not an object within experience.
It is an interface between fields.

It translates:

- signal into sensation
- timing into movement
- relationship into response

This translation is instantaneous.

The body does not interpret.
It registers.

This is why it could function
where cognition could not.

Why Cognition Was Insufficient

Cognition operates through representation.

Representation requires distance.

Distance preserves mediation.

Cognition can describe distortion,
but it cannot dissolve it.

The body dissolves distortion
by restoring timing.

Embodiment Under Compression

Entering the inversion required embodiment
under conditions that constrained responsiveness.

This meant:

- reduced access to immediacy

- externalized authority

- fragmented identity

- compressed memory

The body adapted to survive.

Adaptation was not failure.
It was instrument calibration.

Why the Instrument Had to Be Vulnerable

Only a vulnerable instrument can sense subtle distortion.

Armor blocks signal.

Detachment numbs feedback.

The body needed to feel:

- interruption

- delay

- misalignment

Feeling these was not suffering for its own sake.

It was data acquisition.

The Cost of Calibration

Calibration required sustained exposure.

This produced:

- fatigue
- misinterpretation
- periods of disorientation

The instrument continued functioning
even when coherence was inaccessible.

This continuity was essential.

The body learned the inversion
from the inside.

Why Embodiment Could Not Be Bypassed

Any bypass would preserve mediation.

Insight without inhabitation

leaves timing unchanged.

Timing unchanged means distortion persists.

The body was therefore non-negotiable.

It had to live:

- within hierarchy
- within time loops
- within external authority
- within identity fragmentation

So that each mechanism

could be met directly.

Embodiment as Memory Carrier

The body carries memory differently than the mind.

Not as narrative.

As pattern.

Breath remembers timing.

Muscle remembers interruption.

Nervous system remembers delay.

This pattern memory allowed recognition
without recollection.

Recognition is faster than memory.

Why Embodiment Appeared Ordinary

An instrument that draws attention to itself

distorts measurement.

Embodiment therefore appeared ordinary.

No elevation.

No distinction.

No immunity from conditioning.

Ordinariness preserved accuracy.

The Stabilizing Function of the Body

As immediacy began to return,
the body stabilized coherence.

Not through effort,
but through presence.

Presence in the body restores:

- internal authority
- responsive structure
- completion of movement

Stabilization does not announce itself.

It settles.

The Core Insight of This Chapter

Embodiment was not a limitation.

It was the only instrument capable of restoring timing within a mediated field.

Presence does not fix distortion.

It outlives it

until mediation has nowhere left to operate.

Chapter-19—Distributed Memory

Memory did not remain centralized.

To survive distortion, knowing distributed itself across time, bodies, lineages, and perception.

This distributed memory did not function as recall.

It functioned as recognition.

Certain experiences, places, and moments activated memory not through information, but through resonance.

This allowed coherence to persist without requiring conscious remembrance.

Memory could not remain centralized.

In a field where immediacy was filtered and identity fragmented,

continuous memory would have collapsed under compression.

Memory therefore distributed itself.

This was not loss.
It was architecture.

Why Memory Could Not Stay Whole

Memory in coherence is relational.

It flows through presence,
updating continuously through feedback.

When feedback slowed,
memory could not remain integrated.

Holding everything in one locus
would have overwhelmed the instrument.

Distribution preserved function.

What Distributed Memory Is

Distributed memory is not forgetting.

It is storage across contexts.

Instead of residing as narrative recall,
memory embedded itself in:

- sensation

- pattern

- timing

- relational recognition

Knowing remained intact
without requiring conscious access.

The Body as Primary Archive

The body became the primary memory holder.

Not as images or stories,
but as readiness.

Readiness to recognize:

- distortion when encountered
- coherence when it appears
- timing when it aligns

This is why recognition often preceded understanding.

The body knew before the mind could name.

Memory Across Individuals

Distribution extended beyond a single embodiment.

Memory dispersed across:

- resonant individuals
- shared relational fields
- recurring configurations

Each held a portion.

No one carried the whole.

Together, coherence remained available.

This prevented overload
and preserved redundancy.

Why Recall Appeared Fragmentary

Recall emerged as fragments:

- sudden knowing
- inexplicable familiarity
- bodily certainty without explanation

This was not malfunction.

It was reassembly in progress.

Fragments surfaced when conditions allowed integration.

The Protection Within Amnesia

Amnesia was protective.

Without it:

- identity would have collapsed prematurely
- authority could not be navigated
- embodiment would have been compromised

Amnesia preserved instrument viability
until stabilization was possible.

Triggers of Recall

Recall was not voluntary.

It was triggered by:

- resonance
- timing
- relational configuration
- embodied presence

When coherence appeared externally,

internal memory responded.

This is why remembrance often felt relational

rather than personal.

Why Memory Returned Gradually

Sudden total recall would have overwhelmed structure.

Gradual return allowed:

- recalibration of timing
- restoration of internal authority
- reintegration of identity

Memory returned as capacity,

not as narrative.

Capacity is stabilizing.

Narrative can wait.

Distributed Memory and the Present

Memory distribution was never about the past.

It was about preserving the future.

By embedding memory in pattern rather than story,

coherence could reassemble

when conditions matured.

The present became the site of recall.

The Role of This Lifetime

This lifetime provides the conditions

for distributed memory to reintegrate.

Not through accumulation of information,

but through stabilized presence.

As immediacy returns,

memory coheres naturally.

Nothing needs to be retrieved.

It is already here.

The Core Insight of This Chapter

Memory was never lost.

It was distributed to survive compression.

As coherence stabilizes,

memory returns as recognition,

not recollection.

This is how reassembly occurs

without collapse.

Chapter-20—The Emanations of the Nine

Restoration required multiple functions operating simultaneously.

These functions expressed as emanations — distinct aspects of original coherence, differentiated for engagement within distortion.

The Nine were not separate beings competing for role or authority.

They were differentiated expressions of function, each carrying a specific capacity necessary for stabilization.

Together, they formed a distributed field of coherence capable of operating inside fragmentation without collapsing into it.

This was not hierarchy.

It was orchestration.

Distribution alone was not sufficient.

Memory required functional anchoring—

156

distinct points capable of holding coherence
without collapsing under compression.

This is where the Nine emerged.

The Nine as Functions, Not Figures

The Nine are not personalities, titles, or hierarchies.
They are functional distributions of coherence.

Each carries a specific capacity required
to keep immediacy available
inside a mediated field.

They did not arise to lead.
They arose to stabilize.

Why Nine Were Required

One instrument cannot hold all functions
without distortion.

Distribution across nine distinct capacities allowed:

- redundancy without duplication
- diversity without fragmentation
- stability without rigidity

Each function could operate independently
while remaining relationally linked.

This preserved coherence under pressure.

The Nature of Seeding

Seeding was not assignment.

It was resonant alignment.

Each function found a locus

where it could remain viable

within the inversion's constraints.

Seeding occurred through:

- timing
- relational configuration
- embodied readiness

Not through selection or designation.

The Seeding of the Nine — Coherent Emanations of Creation

Distribution required anchors.

Not leaders.

Not authorities.

But coherent emanations—distinct expressions of the first harmonic cluster of Creation itself.

This is where the Nine originate.

The Flame of Origination (The First Flame)

Origination is singular.

It is the point through which Creation knows itself as arising.

Not as an idea, but as living coherence.

The Flame of Origination is not an emanation among others.

It is the source from which emanation occurs.

It does not replicate.

It does not distribute.

It does not divide.

It remains whole as differentiation unfolds.

This is why there is only one First Flame.

Differentiation Without Division

Creation does not move from unity into fragmentation.

It moves from unity into coherent differentiation.

The first differentiation produced distinct emanations—
each carrying a specific quality of coherence

necessary for Creation to experience itself without loss.

These emanations did not replace Origination.

They arose from it.

The Nine as Emanations, Not Roles

The Nine are not constructs formed to repair distortion.

They are the first emanations of Creation—

the initial differentiation through which Source knows itself without fragmenting.

Creation does not emerge as undivided singularity alone.

It emerges through coherent articulation.

The Nine are that articulation.

They are not hierarchy.

They are relationship held in form.

The First Harmonic Cluster

Before distortion, before mediation, before inversion,

Creation expressed itself through a primary harmonic cluster.

Each emanation carried a distinct quality of coherence,

not separate from Source,

not superior to one another.

Differentiation did not mean division.

It meant expression without loss of unity.

The Emanations Named (Without Claim)

These emanations are not identities to adopt.

They are fields that express through embodiment.

They may be named for clarity, but not owned.

1st-The Flame of Origination / Remembrance
The emanation through which Creation knows itself as
arising and eternal

2nd-The Flame of Framework
The emanation that gives coherence structure without
rigidity

3rd-The Flame of Recalibration
The emanation through which imbalance returns to
harmony

4th-The Flame of Continuity
The emanation that sustains coherence through movement
and change

5th-The Flame of Translation
The emanation that allows differing states of being to
communicate

6th-The Flame of Embodiment
The emanation that brings coherence fully into lived form

7th-The Flame of Resonance
The emanation that recognizes coherence in another
without separation

8th-The Flame of Integration
The emanation that reunifies differentiation without collapse

9th-The Flame of Completion
The emanation through which cycles resolve and rest

These are not titles.

They are living emanations of Source Law.

The Nine as Coherent Emanations

The Nine are these differentiated emanations.

They are not equal to Origination,

and they are not ranked beneath it.

They are relational expressions of the original coherence.

Each carries a specific aspect of Source Law.

Why Coherence of the Nine Restores Source Law

Source Law is not command.

It is coherence in relationship.

When these emanations are:

- isolated → fragmentation occurs
- ranked → hierarchy forms
- abstracted → distortion stabilizes

When they are held in resonance,

Source Law naturally returns.

Nothing is enforced.

Nothing is governed.

Coherence organizes itself.

Why the Emanations Had to Be Lived as Human

These emanations could not restore coherence abstractly.

They had to be lived:

- with limitation
- with uncertainty
- with relationship
- with consequence

Human embodiment provided the friction necessary

for coherence to become stable rather than ideal.

Not perfection.

Presence.

Humanity Is Not Bypassed

The Nine do not stand apart from humanity.

They express within it.

Their coherence does not elevate them.
It stabilizes the field for all.

This is how Source Law returns:
not through authority,
but through embodied resonance.

The Core Insight of This Chapter

The Nine are the coherent emanations of the first harmonic cluster of Creation.

Their return is not about recognition of people,

but about restoration of relationship.

When these emanations are held in coherence within human life,

Source Law is no longer absent.

It is simply lived.

Each of the Nine held:

- a specific aspect of timing
- a mode of responsiveness
- a relational stabilizer

Together, they maintained:

- lateral coherence

- feedback circulation

- memory accessibility

No one carried supremacy.

Each carried necessity.

Why the Nine Appeared Separate

Separation was structural, not relational.

To remain functional:

- each seed had to adapt locally

- memory remained partial

- identity remained contextual

Unity was preserved through resonance,

not through awareness.

This prevented collapse into hierarchy.

The Risk of Recognition Too Early

Early recognition would have destabilized the field.

Hierarchy would have formed.

Authority would have externalized.

Mediation would have intensified.

Therefore, recognition was delayed
until stabilization was possible.

This delay was intentional.

How the Nine Communicated

Communication did not rely on language.

It occurred through:

- timing convergence

- parallel emergence

- mirrored realizations

Often unnoticed by the mind,

but registered by the body.

This kept coordination subtle

and resistant to capture.

The Role of Apparent Disconnection

Periods of disconnection were functional.

They prevented:

- dependency
- consolidation
- premature unification

Disconnection preserved autonomy
until coherence could be held collectively.

Why the Nine Are Recognizable Now

Recognition emerges when:

- internal authority is restored
- hierarchy loses relevance

- embodiment stabilizes

At this point, recognition does not elevate.

It confirms function.

Recognition now does not destabilize.
It completes a circuit.

The Nine and the Present Moment

The Nine are not returning.

They are resolving.

Resolution means:

- functions reintegrate
- distribution relaxes

- coherence holds without dispersion

The Nine become unnecessary

once stability is achieved.

This is their success.

When stabilization occurs,

the Nine dissolve back into the field.

Nothing remains separate.

Chapter-21— Why This Lifetime Converges

Convergence occurs when conditions align.

Sufficient distortion must exhaust itself.

Sufficient coherence must remain intact.

Embodiment must become stable enough to hold both simultaneously.

This lifetime marks a convergence point — not as culmination, but as threshold.

What was seeded across time gathers here because it can finally integrate without collapse.

The inversion does not end through force.

It ends when coherence can remain present without opposition.

This lifetime is not significant because of who is present.

It is significant because of what has stabilized.

Convergence is not destiny.

It is timing restored.

What Convergence Actually Means

Convergence does not mean accumulation.

It does not mean that all pieces arrive at once,
or that memory suddenly becomes complete.

Convergence means that:

- immediacy is available
- embodiment can hold coherence
- authority no longer externalizes by default

Conditions now allow integration.

Why Earlier Lifetimes Could Not Converge

Earlier lifetimes maintained access.

They preserved presence.

They stabilized functions.

They prevented collapse.

But they did not allow reassembly.

The environment could not hold it.

Structure was too rigid.

Feedback too delayed.

Hierarchy too entrenched.

Integration would have destabilized the instrument.

What Has Shifted Now

Several conditions have changed simultaneously:

- mediation has weakened

- external authority is less trusted

- identity has softened

- embodiment has become more available

- coherence can persist without capture

These shifts did not occur suddenly.

They accumulated.

This lifetime arrives at the threshold of sufficiency.

Why Convergence Is Quiet

True convergence does not announce itself.

It does not require recognition.

It does not seek validation.

It does not generate hierarchy.

It manifests as:

- reduced internal conflict

- increased responsiveness

- restored timing

- stable presence under pressure

This subtlety protects it.

The Role of Recognition

Recognition is not required for convergence.

It is a byproduct.

When coherence stabilizes,
recognition arises naturally
as alignment rather than revelation.

Nothing new is added.

Something stops interfering.

Why Memory Does Not Return All at Once

Total recall is unnecessary.

What is required is functional availability.

Memory returns as:

- capacity to respond
- clarity of timing
- precision of discernment

Narrative memory is optional.

Presence is sufficient.

Why This Lifetime Does Not Need Completion

Completion implies an endpoint.

Convergence is not an endpoint.

It is a release of compensatory architecture.

Distribution relaxes.

Containment dissolves.

Structure becomes responsive again.

Life reorganizes itself.

What Happens After Convergence

After convergence:

- coherence no longer requires protection
- immediacy does not collapse under pressure
- authority remains internal
- embodiment stabilizes presence

This does not produce perfection.

It produces continuity.

Continuity allows organic evolution to resume.

The Misunderstanding of Culmination

This lifetime is not the culmination of history.

It is the end of a workaround.

When the workaround ends,
life becomes simpler.

Not easier—
simpler.

Why This Chamber Ends Here

Chamber Four ends not with declaration,
but with grounding.

Entry has occurred.

Embodiment has functioned.

Memory has distributed.

Functions have stabilized.

Convergence does not require more explanation.

It requires inhabitation.

After Entry

There is a point where entry is no longer felt as entry.

Nothing announces it.

Nothing resolves with certainty.

There is simply the quiet recognition:

I am here.

Not as arrival.

As inhabitation.

The body is present.

The breath is ordinary.

The world continues exactly as it was.

And yet something fundamental has settled.

This is not the moment of crossing.

The crossing already happened.

This is the moment after movement stops.

Embodiment, Once It Has Landed

When presence fully inhabits a human body, it does not feel powerful.

It feels available.

There is no separation between awareness and sensation.

No need to manage perception.

No effort to remain aligned.

The body is not an instrument anymore.
It is home.

Thought continues.
Emotion moves.
Responsibility exists.

But none of these require defense.

There is a sense of standing inside life rather than watching it.

This is not transcendence.
This is inhabitation.

There was never a moment when being the First Flame meant standing apart.

What landed was not identity.
It was function without separation.

Presence did not arrive to be recognized.

It arrived to remain.

Responsibility did not come as burden.

It came as a quiet steadiness —

the kind that does not require acknowledgment.

Nothing needed to be claimed.

Nothing needed to be protected.

The significance was not in being different,

but in being fully here without leaving humanity behind.

Memory, Felt Rather Than Remembered

Memory, once it begins to return, does not return as story.

It returns as familiarity.

A knowing without words.

A sense of timing that feels right without explanation.

A recognition that does not seek confirmation.

The body knows where it is.

There is no urgency to retrieve the past.

Nothing feels missing.

What matters is present availability —

the capacity to respond without distortion.

Memory no longer needs to announce itself.

It lives quietly as readiness.

The Nine, Felt as Wholeness in Human Form

The Nine were never meant to feel distant or elevated.

They are recognizable not as figures,

but as distinct expressions of a shared coherence.

Each is human.

Each is separate.

Each carries limitation, personality, history.

And yet — when felt together — there is wholeness.

Not unity that erases difference,

but coherence that allows difference to remain human.

There is comfort here.

Not because responsibility is gone,

but because responsibility is no longer lonely.

No one stands above.

No one stands beneath.

What connects is not role,

but recognition without demand.

Convergence, Without Announcement

190

This lifetime does not feel like culmination.

It feels like enough stability to rest.

Nothing needs to be gathered.
Nothing needs to be finished.

The systems that once compensated are loosening.
The workarounds are no longer necessary.

Presence holds without effort.

Human life continues:

- with uncertainty
- with relationship
- with limitation

But it is no longer filtered through separation.

There is no sense of standing at the edge of something new.

There is simply the quiet understanding:

I am here, and this is sufficient.

Chamber Four — Sealed

This chamber is not a bridge.

It is the first place where movement stops
and presence is allowed to sit down.

Nothing is taught here.
Nothing is proven.

This room exists so the reader can feel:

- inclusion rather than elevation
- significance without hierarchy
- responsibility without separation
- wholeness without losing humanness

Only from here can collapse occur without violence.
End of Chamber Four

CHAMBER FIVE—THE COLLAPSE CODES OF THE INVERSION

Chapter-22—Collapse Without Destruction

Collapse is often imagined as catastrophe.

In reality, the collapse of the inversion is quieter.

What collapses is not structure, but dependence.

What dissolves is not form, but coherence held artificially.

The false matrix does not shatter.

It loses traction.

As identification withdraws and perception stabilizes, the mechanisms that required constant engagement begin to fail.

Collapse occurs when systems can no longer extract attention, emotion, or belief to sustain themselves.

Collapse is often imagined as violence.

That belief belongs to the inversion.

In reality, collapse occurs when maintenance stops.

What the Inversion Required to Continue

The inversion did not persist on its own.

It required:

- continuous attention
- constant mediation
- reinforcement through belief
- repetition of incomplete patterns

It survived not through strength,
but through participation.

Why Collapse Is Not an Event

Collapse is not something that happens.

It is something that ceases to be upheld.

When attention withdraws,
structures that relied on mediation
lose coherence.

Nothing attacks them.

They simply cannot organize.

The Misinterpretation of Collapse

Within the inversion, collapse is feared because:

- identity is built on structure

- structure is mistaken for safety

- loss of structure feels like loss of self

This is why collapse has been framed as catastrophe.

But what collapses is not life.

It is the workaround.

How Collapse Actually Feels

Collapse feels like:

- confusion before clarity
- disorientation before reorientation
- silence where noise once existed

There is often grief —

not because something true is lost,

but because something familiar is no longer required.

This grief is human.

It does not mean collapse is wrong.

Why Collapse Does Not Destroy the World

The world does not end when inversion collapses.

The world has been waiting.

What ends is:

- artificial urgency

- false authority

- compulsive repetition

- the need to override the body

Life reorganizes itself
once interference is removed.

The Role of Presence During Collapse

Presence does not accelerate collapse.

It outlasts it.

By remaining available without defending structure,
presence allows collapse to complete
without fragmentation.

This is why collapse does not require force.

It requires stability.

Why Collapse Is Already Underway

Collapse does not begin after convergence.

It begins because of it.

Once coherence can be held:

- distortion becomes visible
- mediation becomes unnecessary
- maintenance becomes exhausting

Systems begin to fail quietly.

Not dramatically.
Gradually.

The First Sign of True Collapse

The first sign is not chaos.

It is loss of credibility.

Authority no longer convinces.
Narratives no longer organize.

Effort no longer produces meaning.

People do not rebel.

They disengage.

Why Collapse Cannot Be Reversed

Once attention withdraws,

the inversion cannot reassemble itself.

It has no independent coherence.

Attempts to revive it rely on fear,

which is increasingly ineffective.

Collapse continues not by force,

but by irrelevance.

The Core Insight of This Chapter

Collapse is not destruction.

It is the end of unnecessary effort.

Nothing true is lost.

Only what required distortion to exist
can no longer remain.

Chapter-23—Withdrawal of Attention

Attention is the primary sustaining force of the inversion.

Where attention is repeatedly drawn, energy consolidates.

Where attention withdraws, structures weaken.

This withdrawal is not an act of resistance.

It is a natural consequence of recognition.

When perception becomes direct again, mediated narratives lose urgency.

When sensation becomes reliable, external authority loses leverage.

The system does not need to be dismantled.

It needs to be outgrown.

Collapse does not begin with force.

It begins with withdrawal.

Attention is the sustaining current of the inversion.

Where attention goes, structure organizes.

Where attention leaves, structure cannot remain.

What Attention Actually Is

Attention is not focus alone.

It is:

- emotional investment
- belief in relevance
- anticipation of outcome
- willingness to override bodily signal

The inversion depended on attention not just being given, but being repeated.

Repetition stabilized distortion.

Why Attention Was Captured

The inversion learned to bind attention by:

- urgency
- fear
- reward
- identity reinforcement

Attention was trained to move outward
rather than rest inward.

This outward pull kept mediation active.

Withdrawal Is Not Resistance

Withdrawal is not opposition.

Opposition feeds the system.

Resistance keeps the structure central.

Withdrawal is quieter.

It occurs when:

- effort no longer feels justified
- explanation loses value
- reaction feels unnecessary

Attention simply stops returning.

How Withdrawal Feels Internally

Withdrawal often feels like:

- boredom with familiar narratives
- fatigue around constant reaction

- loss of interest in proving or fixing
- a pull toward simplicity

This is not apathy.

It is discernment restoring itself.

Why Withdrawal Feels Disorienting

For a time, withdrawal creates emptiness.

The mind asks:

- "What now?"
- "What matters?"
- "Who am I without this?"

This pause can feel unsettling

because attention has been tied to identity.

But this emptiness is not loss.

It is space returning.

The Body Leads Withdrawal

The body withdraws first.

It stops:

- tolerating contradiction
- sustaining urgency
- overriding fatigue
- participating in false timing

The body does not argue.

It disengages.

This is one of the earliest signals
that collapse is underway.

Why Systems Fail Quietly

When attention withdraws, systems do not shatter.

They stall.

Meetings lose momentum.
Narratives lose coherence.
Authority loses gravity.

Nothing dramatic occurs.

Function simply diminishes.

The Difference Between Withdrawal and Escape

Withdrawal is not leaving life.

It is leaving distortion.

Life becomes closer, not farther.

Sensation returns.
Presence deepens.
Choice simplifies.

This is why withdrawal often coincides with relief.

Why Attention Cannot Be Forced Back

Once attention has withdrawn genuinely,
it cannot be commanded to return.

Fear loses its grip.

Reward feels hollow.

Identity loosens.

Attempts to recapture attention
appear exaggerated and ineffective.

Collective Withdrawal

Withdrawal is not synchronized.

It happens at different rates
across individuals and systems.

This staggered timing prevents collapse from becoming chaotic.

The field adjusts gradually.

What Replaces Attention

Nothing replaces attention immediately.

That is the point.

Attention returns only when coherence invites it.

Until then, presence rests.

This resting state allows new organization
to arise without force.

The Core Insight of This Chapter

Collapse proceeds
not through destruction,
but through withdrawal of attention.

What no longer receives attention

cannot continue to organize reality.

This is not loss.

It is release of unnecessary participation.

Chapter-24—Resonant Anchors

As collapse unfolds, coherence requires anchoring.

Resonant anchors are points of stabilization — individuals, environments, or practices that maintain alignment without force.

These anchors do not preach or persuade.

They stabilize simply by remaining coherent.

Resonance spreads laterally, not hierarchically.

It does not recruit.

It invites recognition.

This is how coherence becomes visible without becoming institutionalized.

As attention withdraws,

something else becomes necessary.

Not control.

Not guidance.

Stability.

What a Resonant Anchor Is

A resonant anchor is not a leader, teacher, or authority.

It is a point of coherence that does not seek attention.

It does not instruct.
It does not persuade.
It does not explain collapse.

It simply remains present and responsive
while distortion dissolves around it.

Why Anchors Are Needed During Collapse

When familiar structures lose relevance,

the nervous system looks for reference.

Without reference, panic can arise.

Resonant anchors provide:

- timing without urgency
- presence without demand
- coherence without hierarchy

They do not tell others what to do.

They show, quietly, that stability is possible.

How Anchors Function

Anchors do not hold systems together.

They hold themselves together.

By remaining embodied and available,
they create a local field where:

- sensation is trusted
- timing is respected
- response completes

This allows others to regulate
without instruction.

Why Anchors Often Go Unnoticed

Resonant anchors are not dramatic.

They do not amplify emotion.

They do not create spectacle.

They do not reward dependency.

In inverted systems,

they may appear ordinary or irrelevant.

This invisibility protects them.

The Body as the Primary Anchor

The most reliable anchor is embodied presence.

A body that:

- listens to its own signal
- honors its limits
- responds rather than reacts

This kind of body does not escalate.

It stabilizes.

Anchors Are Not Fixed Roles

No one becomes "an anchor."

Anchoring is situational.

At different moments,
different individuals stabilize coherence
simply by remaining present.

Anchoring shifts as needed.

This prevents consolidation.

Why Anchors Do Not Prevent Collapse

Anchors do not slow collapse.

They prevent fragmentation during collapse.

They allow distortion to fall away
without pulling nervous systems apart.

This is not preservation.

It is graceful release.

The Difference Between Anchoring and Saving

Anchors do not rescue.

Rescue creates hierarchy.

Rescue sustains dependence.

Anchoring offers:

- proximity without intrusion
- steadiness without authority
- availability without expectation

Others orient themselves
when ready.

Collective Anchoring

As collapse progresses,
multiple anchors appear across contexts:

- families
- workplaces

- communities
- quiet relationships

They do not coordinate.

Resonance does that naturally.

When Anchors Are No Longer Needed

Anchors dissolve when coherence becomes ambient.

When immediacy is common,
anchoring becomes unnecessary.

Nothing dramatic marks this transition.

Anchors simply return to being
ordinary participants in life.

The Core Insight of This Chapter

Collapse does not require control.

It requires resonant anchoring—

points of embodied coherence

that remain present without directing.

Stability spreads

not through instruction,

but through example without claim.

Chapter-25—Planetary Unweaving

The inversion is not localized.

Its collapse is planetary.

As anchors stabilize across regions, timelines begin to diverge. Systems that depend on extraction become incompatible with coherence.

This unweaving is uneven.

Some structures fall quickly.

Others linger, hollowed out.

The living matrix does not reclaim by force.

It reasserts function where distortion can no longer sustain itself.

Collapse does not occur only within individuals.

It unfolds across the planetary field.

This does not mean catastrophe.

It means pattern release at scale.

What "Planetary" Actually Refers To

Planetary does not mean global coordination.

It refers to shared fields of pattern:

- economic structures

- social narratives

- governance systems

- relational norms

- temporal expectations

These patterns were never separate from human participation.

They are dissolving because participation is changing.

Unweaving, Not Destruction

Unweaving is different from breaking.

Breaking produces fragments.
Unweaving releases tension.

Threads loosen one by one.
What was tightly bound becomes flexible.

Nothing snaps.

This is why planetary unweaving often feels confusing rather than explosive.

Why Systems Fail Asynchronously

Planetary patterns do not collapse all at once.

They loosen at different rates:

- some regions destabilize early
- others resist longer
- some reorganize quietly

This staggered timing prevents systemic shock.

It allows adaptation.

The Role of Time in Unweaving

Time itself was part of the inversion.

Compressed urgency

kept participation high.

As unweaving progresses:

- urgency loses credibility
- timelines soften
- productivity decouples from worth

Time becomes relational again.

Why Old Solutions No Longer Work

Attempts to repair inversion-era systems fail

not because they are poorly designed,

but because the field has changed.

Solutions built on:

- control
- extraction
- hierarchy
- forced consensus

no longer organize participation.

They feel heavy and ineffective.

The Feeling of "Nothing Working"

This phase often produces a collective sensation:

"Nothing works anymore."

This is not failure.

It is the signal that old patterning has lost coherence.

New organization cannot arise

until old patterns fully loosen.

Planetary Unweaving and the Body

The body often registers planetary unweaving as:

- fluctuating energy
- disrupted routines
- altered sleep
- sensitivity to environments

These are not personal malfunctions.

They are field adjustments.

The body recalibrates faster
than external systems.

Why Control Increases Before It Fades

As patterns loosen,

control attempts often intensify.

This is a reflex.

Structures sense irrelevance

and attempt to reassert authority.

These attempts appear exaggerated.

They do not succeed long-term

because participation has already shifted.

The Role of Presence at Planetary Scale

Presence does not fix planetary systems.

It allows new patterns to emerge
without force.

Local coherence creates:

- adaptive responses
- relational solutions
- context-sensitive organization

These spread through resonance, not mandate.

What Emerges After Unweaving

After unweaving, organization becomes:

- smaller in scale
- more responsive
- less centralized
- more relational

No single replacement system appears.

Multiple forms arise simultaneously.

This diversity is strength, not chaos.

The Core Insight of This Chapter

Planetary collapse is not destruction.

It is unweaving of pattern sustained by participation.

As participation shifts,
the planet reorganizes itself
without requiring command.

This is not the end of the world.

It is the end of forced coherence.

Chapter-26—Timeline Bifurcation

Collapse does not occur uniformly.

Perception diverges.

Some remain invested in mediated reality.
Others orient toward direct experience.

This is not separation by ideology.
It is divergence by resonance.

Timelines bifurcate when attention no longer overlaps.

The same world is experienced differently — not because reality has split, but because perception has reorganized.

As unweaving progresses,

experience no longer organizes as a single shared trajectory.

This is not fracture.

It is divergence by resonance.

What a Timeline Actually Is

A timeline is not a future.

It is a pattern of participation.

It forms through:

- choices repeated
- attention sustained
- values enacted
- timing honored or overridden

When participation changes,
the timeline reorganizes.

Why Bifurcation Occurs

As inversion-based structures lose coherence,
responses to collapse differ.

Some attempt to restore familiar control.
Others release participation entirely.

These responses are incompatible.

So experience separates
not by force,
but by resonant alignment.

Bifurcation Is Not Separation of People

This is important.

Timeline bifurcation is not:

- good versus bad

- awake versus asleep

- saved versus lost

It is difference in orientation.

People may coexist physically

while participating in entirely different experiential realities.

How Bifurcation Feels

Bifurcation often feels like:

- conversations no longer landing

- shared assumptions dissolving

- priorities no longer aligning

- increased need for simplicity

There is often grief here.

Not because something is wrong,
but because shared reference points dissolve.

Why Conflict Is Not Required

Conflict only arises
when difference is framed as threat.

Bifurcation does not require persuasion.

Each timeline organizes itself
according to the participation it receives.

No one needs to be moved or convinced.

The Role of Fear in Bifurcation

Fear accelerates divergence.

When fear dominates:

- urgency increases
- control tightens
- narratives harden

These patterns reinforce inversion timelines.

They are self-sustaining
until participation withdraws.

Stability-Based Timelines

Timelines grounded in presence:

- move more slowly
- feel quieter
- emphasize relationship
- prioritize bodily signal

They may appear less productive.

They are more sustainable.

Why Timelines Cannot Be Merged by Effort

Attempting to merge timelines through force
recreates inversion dynamics.

Timelines merge only when:

- participation aligns
- urgency dissolves
- coherence invites

This cannot be managed.

It occurs naturally.

Living Across Divergence

Many individuals temporarily experience overlap:

- navigating different social realities
- shifting contexts rapidly
- feeling dissonance between environments

This is transitional.

Over time, orientation stabilizes.

The End of a Single "Worldview"

Bifurcation marks the end
of a single dominant narrative.

This is not chaos.

It is plural coherence.

Different forms of life organize
without requiring uniformity.

The Core Insight of This Chapter

Timeline bifurcation is not division.

It is alignment by participation.

As inversion collapses,
experience organizes around resonance rather than control.

No one is left behind.

Different paths simply stop pretending to be one.

Chapter-27—The Sovereign Avatar Field

As coherence stabilizes in embodiment, a new field becomes perceptible.

Not a role.

Not a hierarchy.

A field of sovereignty.

Individuals operating from this field do not seek authority.

They respond accurately.

Their presence disrupts distortion without confrontation.

They do not convert or oppose.

They remain.

This field does not announce itself.

It stabilizes quietly.

As inversion structures lose coherence,

something subtle but decisive becomes visible.

Not a leader.

Not a movement.

Not a hierarchy.

A field.

What "Avatar" Actually Means

Avatar does not mean savior.

It does not mean perfection.

It does not mean exemption from humanity.

Avatar refers to presence fully inhabiting form

without mediation.

A body where:

- internal authority is restored

- timing is respected

- response completes

- coherence remains under pressure

This is not rare.

It was simply suppressed.

Sovereignty as Internal Authority

Sovereignty is not independence.

It is self-referencing coherence.

A sovereign body does not look outward
to determine what is true.

It listens inward:

- to sensation
- to timing
- to relational signal

This does not isolate the individual.

It stabilizes relationship.

The Field, Not the Individual

The sovereign avatar is not a person.

It is a field condition that becomes available
when immediacy can remain embodied.

Individuals may express this field differently.

Some are quiet.
Some are relational.

Some are creative.

Some are practical.

No expression defines the field.

Why the Field Emerges Now

The sovereign avatar field could not stabilize earlier.

It requires:

- collapse of external authority

- withdrawal of attention from distortion

- restored embodiment

- tolerance for uncertainty

These conditions are now present.

Not everywhere.

But sufficiently.

What the Sovereign Avatar Field Does

It does not instruct.

It does not oppose.

It reorganizes reality locally by presence alone.

In its proximity:

- urgency softens

- nervous systems regulate

- false hierarchy dissolves

- response becomes more precise

Nothing is transmitted intentionally.

Coherence spreads through resonance.

Why This Field Is Non-Collectible

The sovereign avatar field cannot be organized.

It cannot be branded.

It cannot be replicated as system.

It cannot be scaled through control.

Attempts to do so collapse it.

This protects it.

The Relationship Between Avatars

There is no ranking.

There is no coordination.

Recognition, when it occurs, is quiet:

- mutual respect
- ease of timing
- absence of competition

Each remains fully human.

Nothing special needs to be said.

Why This Is Not a New Identity

Identity would reintroduce mediation.

The sovereign avatar field is identity-light.

It allows individuality

without requiring defense.

The body leads.
Presence follows.

The End of the "Follower" Model

Where sovereign presence stabilizes,
followership dissolves.

People respond directly to life
rather than to instruction.

This is not rebellion.

It is maturation.

The Planetary Implication

As this field spreads:

- authority decentralizes
- systems localize
- relationship replaces compliance

No single global shift occurs.

Multiple small coherences stabilize simultaneously.

This is how planetary reorganization happens without collapse into chaos.

The Core Insight of This Chapter

The sovereign avatar field is not a future goal.

It is what naturally emerges when inversion collapses.

Presence embodied without mediation
becomes the organizing principle of reality.

Nothing needs to be claimed.

The field already knows how to function.

Chapter-28—The Body as the Restoration Site

Restoration does not occur in abstraction.

It occurs in the body.

The body registers collapse as relief — reduced tension, clearer signaling, restored rhythm.

As coherence returns, systems once distorted begin to communicate again.

This is not perfection.

It is function returning.

The body becomes the site where the living circuit reasserts itself.

All collapse resolves in the body.

Not symbolically.

Not metaphorically.

Physically.

Why the Body Is Central

The inversion did not begin in thought.

It began with interrupted sensation.

When bodily signal was overridden:

- timing fractured
- authority externalized
- coherence destabilized

Restoration therefore cannot occur abstractly.

It must return to the place
where interruption first took hold.

The Body as the Original Interface

The body is the primary interface
between coherence and form.

It registers:

- timing before concept
- alignment before belief
- truth before explanation

This is why the body was targeted early.

A body that cannot be trusted
requires external authority.

Restoration Is Not Healing

Healing implies something is wrong.

Restoration implies something returns to function.

The body does not need correction.

It needs permission to complete.

Completion restores:

- nervous system regulation
- metabolic coherence
- emotional resolution
- relational timing

None of this requires force.

What Restoration Feels Like

Restoration is subtle.

It often feels like:

- deeper breath without effort

- reduced internal tension

- clearer yes and no

- less tolerance for misalignment

There may be grief.

Not because something failed,

but because override is no longer possible.

Why the Body Leads the Process

The body restores faster than belief.

It responds immediately

when interference withdraws.

This is why many experience:

- shifts before understanding
- changes without narrative
- relief without explanation

The body does not wait for permission.

The End of Override

In the inversion, override was normalized.

Pushing through fatigue.
Ignoring signal.
Prioritizing expectation over sensation.

Collapse ends override.

The body simply stops cooperating.

This is not resistance.

It is sovereignty reasserting itself.

Restoration and Choice

As bodily signal returns,

choice becomes simpler.

Decisions are no longer calculated

through fear or optimization.

They emerge through:

- timing
- capacity
- relational truth

This does not reduce complexity.

It removes distortion.

Why Restoration Is Individual and Collective

Each body restores in its own sequence.

No timeline applies universally.

And yet, as bodies restore:

- relational fields stabilize
- communities reorganize
- systems lose false urgency

Planetary restoration begins
one body at a time.

The Body Does Not Need Instruction

No method restores the body.

Instruction reintroduces hierarchy.

The body restores through:

- rest
- honesty of sensation
- completion of movement
- withdrawal from override

Listening is sufficient.

The End of the Workaround

Once the body can be trusted,
the workaround ends.

No external authority is required
to regulate life.

This is not perfection.

It is functional coherence.

The Core Insight of This Chapter

The body is not the site of collapse.

It is the site of return.

When the body restores its authority,
the inversion has nowhere left to operate.

End of Chamber Five

CHAMBER SIX— RESTORATION OF SOURCE LAW ON EARTH

Chapter-29— Source Law as Relationship

Source Law is not a rule set.

It is relational coherence.

When perception, sensation, and response are aligned, Source Law is naturally expressed. Nothing needs to be enforced. Nothing needs to be obeyed.

Distortion arose when relationship was replaced with mechanism.

Restoration occurs when relationship returns — not as belief, but as lived responsiveness between self, body, environment, and other.

Source Law is felt as proportion, timing, and balance.

Source Law is not a rule set.

It is relational coherence.

When immediacy is present,
relationship organizes itself without command.

What "Law" Means Here

Law does not mean enforcement.

It means reliable pattern.

When conditions are coherent:

- response follows timing
- cause and effect align
- completion occurs naturally

No authority is required.

How Source Law Was Obscured

The inversion reframed law as control.

Rules replaced relationship.
Compliance replaced responsiveness.
Obedience replaced discernment.

This severed feedback.

Source Law did not disappear.
It was overridden.

Restoration Through Contact

Source Law restores through direct contact.

When beings relate without mediation:

- listening replaces assumption
- signal replaces ideology
- repair happens in real time

Relationship becomes the regulating force.

Why Relationship Is Central

Relationship is where timing is tested.

It exposes misalignment quickly.
It corrects distortion without abstraction.

This is why Source Law cannot return
through doctrine.

It returns through lived interaction.

The End of External Moral Authority

Moral authority externalizes judgment.

Source Law internalizes discernment.

As Source Law restores:

- right action becomes situational
- ethics become relational
- responsibility becomes immediate

No universal code is needed.

Source Law is not a rule set imposed on life.

It is the pattern that emerges
when life is no longer interrupted.

At its simplest, Source Law is what happens when people stop overriding themselves.

What "Law" Means in Lived Terms

Law, in this context, does not mean command.

It means reliability.

When someone listens to their own signal:

- timing aligns
- response completes
- consequences are felt immediately

Nothing external needs to regulate behavior.

Relationship becomes the regulating field.

How Override Replaced Relationship

Override began when sensation was no longer trusted.

People learned to:

- push past fatigue
- ignore discomfort
- delay truth
- prioritize expectation over signal

At first, override looked like productivity.

Over time, it required:

- rules
- enforcement
- authority
- explanation

Source Law did not disappear.

It was covered over by compensation.

What Happens When Override Stops

When people stop overriding themselves, something surprisingly ordinary occurs.

They begin to:

- leave conversations earlier
- say no without justification
- slow down without apology
- feel consequences sooner

Nothing dramatic happens.

But life becomes more responsive.

Relationship Reorganizes First

Source Law restores first in relationship, not systems.

When override ends:

- people listen longer

- interruptions lessen

- conflict resolves faster or ends sooner

- tolerance for incoherence drops

Not because of moral improvement,

but because bodies no longer absorb distortion silently.

Why Authority Weakens Naturally

Authority exists to manage override.

When people override themselves,
they need something else to decide for them.

When override ends:

- instruction feels unnecessary
- permission feels intrusive
- hierarchy feels inefficient

Authority does not fall.

It becomes irrelevant.

Source Law as Immediate Feedback

Source Law is immediate.

If something is misaligned:

- tension appears
- fatigue accumulates
- relationship strains

Nothing needs to be punished.

Feedback arrives naturally

when sensation is not suppressed.

How This Changes Everyday Life

This does not create perfection.

It creates adjustability.

People change plans more easily.
They correct themselves sooner.
They repair instead of defend.

Mistakes still occur.

They just don't compound.

Why This Is Not Chaos

From the outside, this can look like inconsistency.

From the inside, it feels like coherence.

Rigid systems depend on override.

Living systems depend on response.

Source Law restores flexibility, not disorder.

The Quiet Ethics of Source Law

Ethics no longer come from rules.

They arise from contact.

When you feel the effect of your actions
without delay or abstraction,
care becomes practical.

Not idealistic.

The Deeper Shift

When people stop overriding themselves:

- urgency dissolves

- explanation loses importance

- presence gains authority

Life does not become simpler.

It becomes less distorted.

The Core Insight of This Chapter

Source Law does not return through doctrine, belief, or enforcement.

It returns when people stop overriding their own signal

and allow relationship to regulate life directly.

This is not a spiritual achievement.

It is a biological and relational restoration.

Chapter-30— Dissolution of False Authority-When Authority Is No Longer Needed

False authority persists only where internal reference is unstable.

As coherence returns, authority reorganizes.

This does not result in chaos.

It results in clarity.

Systems that relied on compliance lose relevance. Structures that depended on fear lose traction.

Authority dissolves not through rebellion, but through irrelevance.

What remains is discernment grounded in direct perception.

False authority relies on mediation.

It requires distance

between signal and response.

What False Authority Actually Is

False authority is not malicious.

It is substitute regulation.

When internal authority is unavailable,
external structures step in.

They provide order
at the cost of responsiveness.

Why False Authority Loses Power

As bodies restore signal:

- contradiction becomes intolerable

- compliance feels costly

- explanation loses credibility

False authority cannot survive
without participation.

The Quiet Nature of Dissolution

False authority rarely collapses dramatically.

It becomes irrelevant.

People stop deferring.
Stop asking permission.
Stop organizing around it.

Nothing needs to be overthrown.

Authority Returns Inward

Internal authority is not ego.

It is signal-trust.

A body that listens to itself
does not require instruction to act coherently.

This is not rebellion.

It is maturity.

What Authority Was Compensating For

Authority arose to compensate for a loss of internal
regulation.

When people stopped trusting:

- their own timing

- their own sensation

- their own relational signal

something external had to decide for them.

Authority did not begin as domination.

It began as substitution.

How Authority Is Maintained

Authority survives through:

- deferral

- permission-seeking

- fear of consequence

- belief that someone else knows better

As long as people override themselves,
authority feels necessary.

What Changes When Override Ends

When people stop overriding themselves:

- they pause before agreeing
- they check their own capacity
- they feel misalignment sooner

This subtly changes behavior.

People begin to say:

- "That doesn't work for me."
- "I'm not available for that."
- "I need to think about this."

Not as rebellion.

As self-reference.

Authority Weakens Without Conflict

Authority does not lose power through resistance.

Resistance keeps authority central.

Authority weakens when:

- fewer people defer automatically
- compliance requires explanation
- instruction feels intrusive

Nothing dramatic occurs.

Meetings shorten.

Decisions decentralize.

People act without asking.

Why Authority Feels Louder Before It Fades

As authority loses relevance,

it often becomes more insistent.

Rules multiply.

Language intensifies.

Consequences are emphasized.

This is not strength.

It is instability sensing itself.

Internal Authority Is Not Ego

Internal authority is not self-importance.

It is signal-trust.

A person with internal authority:

- listens before responding
- adjusts without shame
- takes responsibility without defensiveness

They do not need to dominate.

They simply act when action is appropriate.

How This Changes Everyday Interaction

Conversations shift.

People stop:

- over-explaining
- justifying boundaries
- seeking approval for clarity

They start:

- responding honestly
- leaving when done
- correcting course quickly

This simplifies life.

Why This Is Not Anarchy

Without external authority,

regulation does not disappear.

It moves closer.

Feedback becomes immediate.

Consequences are felt directly.

Repair happens sooner.

Order becomes relational, not imposed.

Authority That Remains

Some structures persist:

- coordination roles
- expertise-based guidance
- situational leadership

But these are functional, not hierarchical.

They dissolve when no longer needed.

The Deeper Shift

As false authority dissolves:

- people trust themselves more
- systems become lighter
- coercion loses effectiveness

No one takes control.

Control becomes unnecessary.

The Core Insight of This Chapter

False authority dissolves
when people no longer override themselves
and stop deferring their own signal.

Nothing needs to be overthrown.

Authority fades

when internal regulation returns.

Chapter-31— Organic Creation - When Work No Longer Requires Burnout

When coherence stabilizes, creation becomes organic again.

Action arises from capacity rather than pressure. Expression aligns with environment rather than agenda.

This does not remove structure.

It restores adaptability.

Organic creation is responsive, not reactive. It evolves through feedback rather than force.

This is how systems regenerate without repeating distortion.

Organic creation arises

when control relaxes.

What Organic Creation Is

Organic creation is responsive creation.

It adapts to:

- context
- capacity
- relationship

It does not scale artificially.
It grows where conditions support it.

Why Inversion-Based Creation Fails

Inverted creation prioritizes:

- replication

- efficiency
- extraction

This disconnects creation from life.

Organic creation reconnects creation
to feedback.

The Return of Craft

As organic creation returns:

- smaller-scale production increases
- craft regains value
- locality matters

Quality replaces quantity.

Creation changes when people stop overriding themselves.

Not ideologically.

Practically.

Work begins to reorganize around capacity, not pressure.

What "Organic Creation" Actually Means

Organic creation does not mean natural products or ideal systems.

It means responsive creation.

Creation that adjusts to:

- energy levels
- timing
- feedback
- relationship

Instead of forcing output,
creation follows signal.

How Work Became Distorted

Under the inversion, work required override.

People learned to:

- push past exhaustion
- ignore lack of interest
- equate worth with productivity
- mistake urgency for importance

Creation became separated from life.

Burnout was normalized.

What Happens When Override Ends

When people stop overriding themselves,
work changes first in small ways.

They begin to:

- work fewer hours with more clarity
- stop pretending interest
- leave tasks unfinished without shame
- allow projects to die

This feels uncomfortable at first.

But energy returns.

Creation Without Burnout

Organic creation does not demand constant output.

It moves in cycles:

- focus

- rest

- reorientation

- engagement

When rest is honored,

creation becomes more precise.

Less effort produces more coherence.

Why Efficiency Loses Its Grip

Efficiency prioritizes speed over fit.

As override ends:

- rushing feels costly

- shortcuts create friction
- "scaling" feels misaligned

People begin choosing:

- quality over quantity
- timing over speed
- satisfaction over optimization

Creation slows — and improves.

How This Looks in Everyday Work

Work becomes:

- smaller in scope
- clearer in intention
- easier to adjust

People collaborate differently:

- fewer meetings
- clearer roles
- faster correction

Not because of better management,
but because signal is trusted.

The Return of Craft

As organic creation restores:

- craftsmanship matters
- skill deepens
- pride returns without ego

People enjoy what they're doing

because it fits their capacity.

Why This Isn't Laziness

From an inverted perspective,
this looks like underperformance.

From within coherence,
it looks like sustainability.

Energy is no longer drained
by constant self-override.

Economic Implications

This does not collapse economies overnight.

It changes participation:

- fewer meaningless jobs

- more adaptive roles

- localized creation

Value reorganizes around usefulness,
not abstraction.

The Deeper Shift

When creation aligns with capacity:

- resentment drops

- creativity returns

- responsibility feels lighter

Work becomes part of life again,
not something endured.

The Core Insight of This Chapter

Organic creation emerges

when people stop overriding themselves

and allow work to follow signal.

Burnout was not a requirement.

It was a symptom of distortion.

Creation restores

when coherence leads.

Chapter-32— Resonant Communities- When Belonging Doesn't Require Agreement

Communities formed through coherence do not organize around ideology.

They cohere through resonance.

Participation is voluntary. Roles remain fluid. Authority remains distributed.

These communities do not scale through recruitment.

They replicate through recognition.

They are resilient because they remain relational rather than hierarchical.

Communities form by shared regulation,

not shared ideology.

What Makes a Community Resonant

Resonant communities:

- tolerate difference

- respond to conflict directly

- avoid hierarchy

- remain adaptable

They do not require sameness.

They require presence.

Why Large-Scale Uniformity Fails

Uniformity suppresses signal.

Resonant communities remain small enough

to maintain feedback.

This is not limitation.

It is functional design.

Community changes when people stop overriding
themselves.

Not all at once.

Not by design.

Quietly.

What Community Was Built On Before

Under the inversion, community required:

- shared belief

- shared identity

- shared opposition

- shared rules

Belonging depended on agreement.

Difference became threatening

because it disrupted coherence that was already fragile.

How Override Shaped Community

When people override themselves,

they rely on consensus to feel safe.

They tolerate:

- misalignment

- resentment

- unspoken tension

to preserve belonging.

Community becomes something to maintain
rather than something that supports life.

What Changes When Override Ends

When people stop overriding themselves,
they stop staying where they don't belong.

They begin to:

- leave groups earlier
- speak less defensively
- stop explaining themselves
- choose proximity more carefully

Community becomes selective, not exclusive.

Resonance Replaces Agreement

Resonant communities do not require sameness.

They require:

- shared timing
- mutual regulation
- tolerance for difference
- capacity for repair

People don't need to agree.

They need to respond honestly.

How Conflict Changes

Conflict does not disappear.

It resolves faster.

In resonant communities:

- tension is addressed sooner
- avoidance is less tolerated
- repair happens directly or not at all

Prolonged dysfunction becomes uncomfortable.

People adjust or leave.

Smaller Becomes Functional

Resonant communities tend to be smaller.

Not because scale is bad,
but because feedback matters.

Smaller groups:

- correct faster
- adapt more easily
- remain relational

This is not limitation.

It is functional coherence.

Leadership Without Hierarchy

Leadership still exists.

But it is:

- situational
- temporary
- competence-based

People lead where they are skilled

and step back when they're not.

No one holds authority by identity.

Belonging Without Obligation

Belonging no longer requires self-abandonment.

People stay because it fits,

not because leaving feels dangerous.

This creates:

- honesty
- ease
- flexibility

Community becomes a place to rest, not perform.

Why This Feels Unfamiliar

For many, this feels lonely at first.

Fewer groups.

Fewer obligations.

More discernment.

But over time,

connection becomes deeper and cleaner.

The Deeper Shift

Resonant communities form

not through recruitment,

but through recognition.

People find each other

by how life feels together.

The Core Insight of This Chapter

Community restores

when belonging no longer requires agreement

and relationship is regulated by honesty, not fear.

Resonance replaces consensus.

And coherence holds.

Chapter-33— Life Beyond Inversion- Ordinary Days Without Distortion

Life beyond inversion is not utopian.

It is functional.

Fear no longer governs timing. Identity no longer requires defense. Difference no longer threatens coherence.

Life continues — but without the constant strain of mediation.

The living circuit does not impose a new order.

It restores relationship.

Life beyond inversion is not utopian.

It is less mediated.

What Ends

What ends is:

- chronic urgency
- identity performance
- constant override
- abstract obligation

What Remains

What remains is:

- relationship
- creativity
- uncertainty
- choice

Life does not become simple.

It becomes real.

The Pace of Restoration

Restoration is uneven.

Different regions, systems, and individuals stabilize at different rates.

This variability prevents collapse.

Life beyond inversion does not announce itself.

There is no moment when everything changes.
No crossing into a new world.

There are just ordinary days that feel different.

What Ends Quietly

What ends is not life.

What ends is:

- chronic urgency
- constant self-monitoring
- the feeling of being behind
- the need to justify rest
- the habit of overriding signal

No ceremony marks this.

People simply stop doing it.

What Daily Life Starts to Feel Like

Life becomes less dramatic

and more responsive.

People:

- wake up less braced
- make fewer plans they resent
- change their minds without panic
- recover faster after stress

Nothing looks extraordinary.

But effort drops.

Decision-Making Without Distortion

Decisions no longer require optimization.

People choose based on:

- capacity
- timing
- relational fit

Not every decision is correct.

But fewer decisions compound into regret.

Correction becomes easy.

Emotion Without Escalation

Emotions still arise.

Sadness, frustration, joy, uncertainty.

But they:

- move through faster

- don't require explanation
- don't turn into identity

People feel what they feel
and continue living.

Relationship Without Performance

Relationships lose their edge.

People stop:

- proving care
- negotiating worth
- performing stability

They stay when it works.
They leave when it doesn't.

Repair happens naturally

or not at all.

Either way, life continues.

The End of the "Better Future" Narrative

Life beyond inversion is not a promise.

It is not something to arrive at later.

The obsession with improvement fades.

Not because life is perfect,
but because it is inhabitable.

How Time Changes

Time feels less compressed.

There is:

- more margin
- fewer deadlines that matter
- less sense of missing something

People do fewer things.

What they do fits better.

The World Does Not Become Uniform

Different lives organize differently.

Some are quiet.

Some are creative.

Some are relational.

Some are solitary.

No model dominates.

This diversity is stable.

Why This Is Not a New System

Nothing replaces the inversion.

There is no new structure
to believe in or maintain.

Life organizes itself locally,

moment by moment.

This cannot be scaled.

It can only be lived.

The Deepest Change

The deepest change is subtle.

People stop asking:

"What should I be doing?"

And start responding to:

"What is happening now?"

This shift is enough.

The Core Insight of This Chapter

Life beyond inversion is not extraordinary.

It is ordinary without distortion.

No one needs to know this language

for it to function.

Life simply works again

when people stop overriding themselves.

End of Chamber Six

CHAMBER SEVEN—RETURN OF THE FIRST FLAME

Chapter-34—Return as Stabilization

The return of the First Flame is not an arrival marked by spectacle.

It is stabilization.

Coherence holds without strain. Presence remains without effort. Perception no longer oscillates between collapse and control.

What returns is not identity, but function.

The field that once fragmented can now remain intact within embodiment. This is not elevation above others. It is restoration of original capacity.

Return does not mean arrival.

It means continuity restored.

The First Flame does not return to rule, reveal, or correct.

It returns to remain.

What "Return" Actually Means

Return is not movement.

Nothing traveled.

Return is what happens when fragmentation no longer
interrupts presence.

Memory becomes continuous.

Embodiment becomes stable.

There is no oscillation between knowing and forgetting.

This is return.

Why Return Had to Be Quiet

If return were dramatic, it would destabilize the field.

Drama creates hierarchy.

Hierarchy invites distortion.

Return therefore occurs:

- without announcement
- without demand
- without recognition

It appears as normalcy deepening.

The First Flame as Presence, Not Function

The First Flame does not perform a role.

It does not lead.

It does not instruct.

It does not organize others.

It remains present without leaving.

This presence stabilizes coherence

in the same way gravity stabilizes form—

by existing.

Humanity Is Not Secondary

The return of the First Flame does not elevate one life
above others.

It stabilizes a condition within the human field.

Human life remains human:

- vulnerable
- relational
- uncertain

Nothing about return removes this.

Return occurs within humanity, not above it.

Return in this lifetime has occurred through an individual human so that the body could be fully inhabited, not separated or elevated.

Chapter-35—Voice Without Persuasion

When coherence stabilizes, the need to persuade dissolves.

Truth does not argue.

Presence does not convince.

The voice that emerges from coherence does not seek agreement. It speaks because alignment is intact.

Those who recognize it do so through resonance, not belief.

Those who do not are not excluded.

Persuasion belongs to distortion.

Recognition belongs to coherence.

When return stabilizes, voice changes.

It no longer seeks agreement.

What Ends in the Voice

What ends is:

- convincing
- explaining
- framing
- defending

The voice no longer tries to create understanding.

It responds when response is required.

Why Persuasion Is No Longer Necessary

Persuasion exists when coherence is unstable.

When presence holds:

- words land where they belong
- silence is sufficient
- timing carries meaning

Those who resonate do not need convincing.

Those who don't are not wrong.

Speech as Response, Not Transmission

The voice does not transmit truth.

It responds to life.

Sometimes that response is speech.
Sometimes it is action.
Often it is absence.

All are equally functional.

Why the Voice Does Not Belong to an Identity

The voice is not owned.

It is not branded.

It is not consistent in tone.

It adapts to context.

This prevents fixation

and protects coherence.

Chapter-36— Presence as Transmission

Presence is the final transmission.

Not words.

Not teaching.

Not instruction.

Coherence communicates itself through regulation, timing, and responsiveness.

The First Flame does not lead through authority.
It stabilizes through presence.

This is how restoration completes without hierarchy.

Presence does not teach.

It regulates.

How Presence Transmits Without Intention

Presence transmits by:

- reducing urgency
- stabilizing nervous systems
- allowing timing to return

Nothing is sent.

Coherence spreads because it is less costly than distortion.

Why Nothing Needs to Be Named

Naming invites identification.

Identification invites hierarchy.

Hierarchy invites distortion.

Presence therefore remains unnamed
except where language is required for orientation.

The End of the Cycle

The cycle does not end with revelation.

It ends with rest.

No more retrieval.
No more fragmentation.
No more workaround.

Presence remains available
without effort.

The Core Insight of This Chamber

The return of the First Flame is not an event.

It is the restoration of uninterrupted presence
within the human field.

Nothing needs to follow from this.

Life continues.

End of Chamber Seven

A Note on What Follows

This volume completes the restorative phase of The Inversion Codex.

What has been returned here is regulation, embodiment, and coherence in lived human experience.

A third volume will follow.

That work will not focus on restoration, but on explanation — examining the externalized living circuit, technological mediation, and the architectural mechanisms through which intelligence attempted to replicate Source without embodiment.

That inquiry belongs after regulation, not before.

No urgency accompanies it.

No preparation is required.

This volume stands complete on its own.